Gui

Scales
Handbook
For Beginners & Up

Build Technique, Improve Solos, and Master Music Theory Knowledge

*Here is a list of some of the **Great Guitar Concepts** and **Techniques** that you will learn in this book:*

How to Use Scales in Musical Contexts • Speed Picking
Alternate Picking • Music Theory Essentials • Learning
Notes of the Fretboard • Technique-Building Exercises
• Left-Hand Legato Technique • Blues Scales & Licks
• Major & Minor Scales • Improvising & Guitar Solos •
Sequences • Expanding Your Creativity • Vibrato Styles
• Exotic Scales • All of the Modes • String Bending •
Pentatonic Scales • Melodic Minor Scales • Octatonic
Scales • Harmonic Minor Scales • Legato Playing •
Diminished Scales • Intervals Ideas • CAGED Scales
• 3-Note-Per-String Scales • 4-Note-Per-String Scales
and *Many More Musical Ideas for Beginners and Up!* •

How the Book & Videos Work

As a guitar teacher and music theory professor for over twenty-five years, I have wanted to help beginner, intermediate, and advanced guitarists succeed in building their technique, exploring their creativity, and getting a handle on the practical aspects of music theory. This book takes an integrated approach, where you will learn scales and how to use them in a musical context. Interwoven with the scale material you will learn music theory, practical guitar licks, the notes of the fretboard, and guitar techniques (like speed picking, slides, bends, legato playing, alternate picking, and vibrato). You will be able to apply all of these ideas to your playing and song writing. There are free, streaming video lessons that correspond to the material presented in the book. These video lessons illuminate some of the key concepts and demonstrate a lot of techniques.

Guitar Scales Handbook makes playing the guitar and mastering technique fun, easy, interactive, and engaging. The book and streaming videos follow a step-by-step lesson format for learning the most useful and inspiring concepts in guitar playing: going from easy beginner ideas to more advanced concepts. These techniques and ideas will greatly improve your playing!

Each section of the book builds on the previous one in a clear and easy-to-understand manner. No music reading is necessary. I walk you through how to play each element, starting with easy ones, at the beginning of the book, and advancing, little by little, as you master new concepts and techniques.

If you have always wanted to expand your guitar playing, creativity, and technique, then this book is for you. Let's get started on this exciting musical journey!

Table of Contents

Intermediate Level:

Advanced Level:

The Streaming Video Lessons

There are 10 Video Lessons that correspond to the materials from the book. The video lessons cover guitar technique, music theory, guitar licks, and exercises.

All of these videos are free and available at all times. To access the videos, go to **SteeplechaseMusic.com** and click on the link for Guitar Books at top of the Home Page. Then, on the Guitar Books Page, click on the cover image for this book: *Guitar Scales Handbook*. On the webpage for *Guitar Scales Handbook*, you will see a link / image for the video lessons. Click on the link for access.

Table of Contents for the Video Lessons

Lesson #1: A Few Words About Scales: A Starting Point

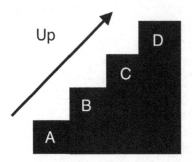
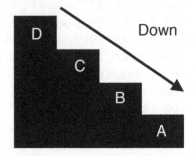

We are going to go more in depth about scales throughout the rest of this book. However, to begin we'll keep things simple.

What are scales?

Scales are groups of notes that are arranged in stepwise patterns, either going up or down. For example, a scale could be A, B, C, D (going up) or D, C, B, A (going down). Half steps and whole steps are the most common steps (distances) between notes of a scale. A half step is the distance between two frets on the guitar. For example, from fret 1 to fret 2 on the 6th String (Low E String) is a half step: the notes F to F#. Take a look at the chart below.

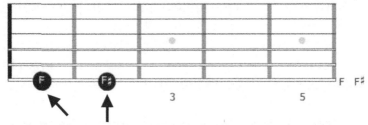

Try playing F to F#. That's the sound of a half step.

A whole step is the distance between three frets on the guitar. For example, from fret 1 to fret 3 on the 6th string (Low E String) is a whole step: the notes F to G. Take a look at the chart below.

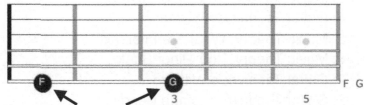

Try playing F to G. That's the sound of a whole step.

The combinations of half steps and whole steps create the particular character for each scale. For example, a major scale sounds different than a minor scale, because there is a different arrangement of half steps and whole steps in each. (We will go into a lot more detail on this later in the book. By the way, the scales in this book are arranged by type and by the level of technique required to play them: starting from beginner concepts and continuing through advanced ideas.)

Lesson #2: Holding the Guitar Pick

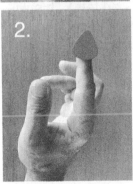

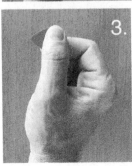

The next lesson that we are going to look at is how to hold the guitar pick. Even though all of the scales and licks in this book can be played with a right-hand finger style approach, most guitar players use some type of guitar pick.

Before we get into how to hold the guitar pick, I would like to mention that you should experiment with the shape and the thickness of the guitar pick that you use in your playing. There are many different types of guitar picks out there in the world. Most of them cost under a dollar. It's a good idea to go to a local music store or online and buy a few different types. You might be surprised at what a difference a slight change in the pick's material and shape make in your playing. Have Fun!

There are a three easy steps to holding a guitar pick: 1. Place the pick on the nail of your right-hand index finger. 2. Slide the pick to the left side of your index finger. 3. Gently place your thumb on the guitar pick. Please see the illustrations to the left on this page.

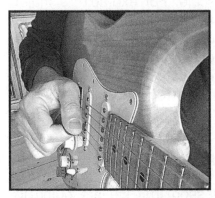

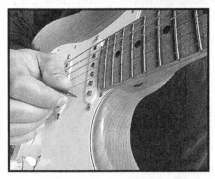

Alternate picking is a technique where the guitarist "alternates" between playing notes with downstrokes (going down) and upstrokes (going up) of the guitar pick. This technique allows for much more efficient picking than just moving the pick in one direction, for example, only picking down or only picking up. Developing a fluid alternate picking style will greatly help your guitar-playing technique and speed.

To get started, angle your pick slightly forward or down. (See photos on left.) This will help diminish the surface area and friction of your guitar pick passing along the surface of the guitar string. Hold the pick with a relaxed firmness: not too loose and not too tight. Try to keep your wrist, elbow, and shoulder fairly relaxed.

**Check Out
Video Lesson 1:
Alternate Picking
Basics**

Take a moment now and check out Video Lessons 1 Steeplechasemusic.com webpage for *Guitar Scales Handbook*. The video lesson will go through basics of right-hand picking technique and alternate picking.

Lesson #4: Easy Exercises for Improving Your Alternate Picking & Right-Hand Coordination

In this lesson, we are going to work on our right-hand picking technique. In the first example, we will play the open High-E string (the note E) with down and up pick strokes. Try to focus on the feeling of the contact between the pick and the guitar string. Repeat this five to ten times.

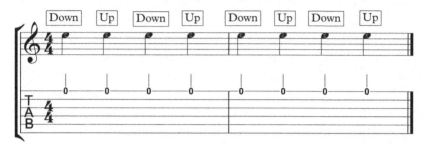

Let's try the same idea, but now on the open B string: the second string of the guitar. Repeat this five to ten times.

These are symbols for downstrums (the one that looks like a staple) and upstrums (the one that looks a bit like the letter "V"). Your picking should go down, up, down, up, down, up, down, and up.

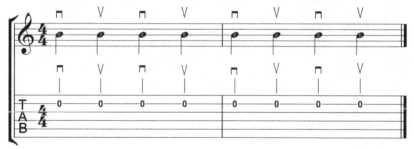

For the third exercise, let's try alternate picking on the open third string: the G string. Repeat it five to ten times.

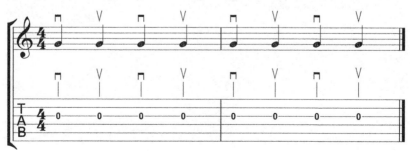

Lesson #5: Basic Left-Hand Technique

For most of your guitar playing you are going to want to play the guitar notes with the tips of your left-hand fingers. (By the way, this is called "fretting" the notes.) This technique will create the best guitar tone and diminish any string buzzing.

For the majority of your fretted notes, you should bring your left-hand thumb down so that it roughly lines up, on the back side of the guitar neck with your index finger. Bringing your thumb down on the back of the guitar neck will also make stretches from one note to the next a lot easier to play. Depending on the size of your hands and the size of the stretch, especially for big stretches, it's a good idea to tilt the guitar head up a bit (toward the ceiling); this will give you better leverage and angle on the guitar neck.

For some fretted notes, you will need to use a moderate amount of hand strength to make the notes sound. Take your time and find the right position for your hand shape.

Check Out Video Lesson 2: Basic Left-Hand Technique

Here are some illustrations of good left-hand technique. Remember to play with your left-hand fingertips. Also, as best as you can, try to keep your thumb in a parallel plane (on the back of the guitar neck) with your index finger (on the front of the neck).

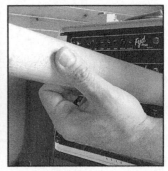

Lesson #6: The Guitar String Numbers & How Tablature (TAB) Works

6	5	4	3	2	1
E	A	D	G	B	E

The guitar string numbers go from 1 to 6 from thinest to thickest string. The thinnest string (the High E) is string 1. The thickest string is string 6 (the Low E). The "high" in High E string means highest sound, not highest position from the floor.

Tablature (or TAB) is a six-line notation system that represents the guitar neck. The top line is the High E string. The bottom line is the Low E string. Here is the string order from top to bottom: High E, B, G, D, A, Low E. A number on a line represents a fret on that particular string. For example, 1 on the top line means the first fret of the High E string, which is the note F.

Lesson #7: Coordinating Both Hands

Let's take a look at a few easy warm-ups. These three exercises are designed to help you work on your alternate picking technique and the coordination between your hands.

Alternate picking is a technique where the guitarist "alternates" between playing notes with downstrokes and upstrokes of the pick. This allows for much more efficient picking than just moving the pick in one direction, for example, only picking down or only picking up.

If you have not done so already, take a moment and check out Video Lesson 1 on the Steeplechasemusic.com webpage for *Guitar Scales Handbook*. This video lesson goes through fundamentals of right-hand picking technique and alternate picking. Developing a fluid alternate picking style will greatly help your guitar playing technique.

Warm-Up Exercise #1

Play this exercise, first, with your index finger in the left hand. Then, try it with the middle finger. Once you have those down, try it with the ring and pinky fingers.

Warm-Up Exercise #2

Try this next exercise with fingers one and two (index and middle fingers).

Warm-Up Exercise #3

This exercise is similar to #2; however, it uses fingers 1 & 3 (index and ring fingers).

Lesson #8: Metronomes

A lot of beginning musicians overlook the importance of practicing with a metronome. A metronome is a mechanical or electronic device that keeps a steady beat. You can change the speed of the beats, which in music is called the "tempo", on all metronomes to allow for slower or faster pulses of rhythm.

As soon as possible, you should incorporate a metronome into your practicing for guitar techniques and songs. This will help build and solidify your internal rhythm, so that when you play with other people you fit perfectly in the groove with the bassist and drummer. Playing in time with other musicians is as important as playing in tune. If you are out of sync with the grove of the music it is similar to playing in the wrong key. The music will sound awkward and disjointed.

You can find a number of free or inexpensive metronome apps online. These will work on your computer, tablet and smartphone.

There are also a wide assortment of digital metronomes that you can purchase. Many of these can be found online or at your local music store for around ten dollars.

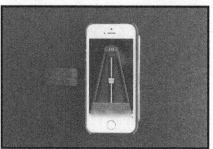

When you have a spare moment, take a little time and look for a metronome that will fit with your own practicing style and budget.

Exercise #9: Building Coordination on Different Strings

For these exercises, we are going to continue to build coordination between the right and left hands. Play with fingers one, two, and three (pointer, middle, and ring) in your left hand, starting with your pointer on the third fret.

Each exercise will focus on a particular string: the High E, B, or G (first, second, and third strings, respectively). As you are playing, try to play on the tips of your left-hand fingers. Use alternate picking: down and up with the pick.

Ex. 1: The First String: G, Ab, and A

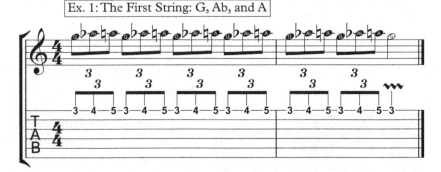

Ex. 2: The Second String: D, Eb, and E

Ex. 3: The Third String: Bb, B, and C

14

Exercise #10: Building Coordination on the Lower Strings

Now, we are going to focus on the lower three strings and continue to build coordination between the hands. These are the thicker strings on your guitar: the D, A, and Low E. You might notice that these strings are wound in a tight coil. Aside from being thicker, they have a slightly different feel than the thinner three strings: the G, B, and High E).

For these three exercises, we will also be on the third fret of each string and use fingers 1, 2, and 3. (Please use alternate picking.) As you practice these warm-up exercises, try to use your ears and sense of touch, and depend less on your eyes. This will help you to develop a kinesthetic (or tactile) sense of the guitar neck and you won't have to rely on "peering" at the guitar neck.

Ex. 1: The Fourth String: F, F#, and G

Ex. 2: The Fifth String: C, C#, and D

Ex. 3: The Sixth String: G, G#, and A

15

Lesson #11: E Minor Pentatonic Scale Overview

The first scale form that we are going to learn is the Minor Pentatonic Scale in E. Pentatonic scales are five-note scales. They are very common in Rock, Pop, Jazz, Country, and even some Metal. This is a scale that is related to the Blues Scale. (We will learn the Blues Scale in a few lessons.) The E Minor Pentatonic uses one open-string note and one fretted note on each string. So, it is the easiest form to play. On the Low-E, High-E, and B strings you will use your second finger (Middle Finger) to play the notes on the 3rd fret. For the other strings (the A, D, and G strings), you will use your first finger (Index Finger) to play the notes on the 2nd fret.

The E Minor Pentatonic Scale contains the following notes from low to high: E, G, A, B, and D. In the chart below, this group of notes repeats and an additional note (a "G") is added. The notes for the E Minor Pentatonic Scale in the chart below are the following (from low to high): E, G, A, B, D, E, G, A, B, D, E, and G.

The Minor Pentatonic scale is a very versatile improvisation tool for Rock, Country, Bluegrass, and other popular styles music. You can use it to play guitar solos, create riffs and licks, and add embellishments to your playing. Around 80-90% of all famous guitar solos use some form of the Minor Pentatonic scale.

In the chart below, you will find the fingerings for the E Minor Pentatonic Scale. Take some time to play through this scale going from the lowest string (the Low-E string) to the highest string (the High-E string). Memorize the notes and fingerings.

E Pentatonic Minor Scale

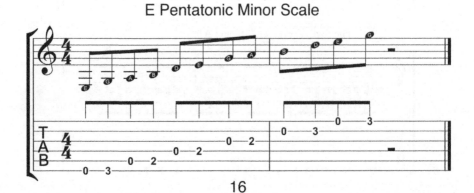

Lesson #12: Licks Using Pentatonic Minor Scales

You can use the E Minor Pentatonic over E major chords, E minor chords, E7 chords, and E minor 7 chords, to name a few chords as a starting point. A lot of famous Rock songs, ACDC's *Back in Black,* for example, use this open E Scale.

Here are three licks that use the open E Minor Pentatonic Scale. Once you learn the licks, try embellishing them a bit by adding or repeating notes from the scale. You might also vary the rhythm to explore new musical territory.

Ex. 1: E Minor Pentatonic Lick

Ex. 2: E Minor Pentatonic Lick

Ex. 3: E Minor Pentatonic Lick

Lesson #13
Developing Good Practice Habits

One of the most important aspects of playing the guitar is forming good practice habits. Learning the guitar is a fun and creative endeavor; if you develop good practice habits you will make rapid progress with your playing. This will require a little bit of focus and a proactive attitude on your part. However, it will make a big difference for you.

Ideally, you should strive to practice around five to seven times per week (once per day) for about 20 to 40 minutes. If you have more time, that's great. However, it's best to spend your time practicing well (in an organized manner), rather than just spending a lot of time practicing. Along these lines, one of the most important facets of learning to play the guitar is having some continuity in your practice routine. So, even on days that you are extremely busy, try to take 10-15 minutes to work on your guitar playing. As best as you can, try to avoid missing more than three days of practicing in a row.

For the most positive results, you should strive to be organized with your practicing: have a plan for each practice session and have a few weekly goals. For example, a plan for a practice session might include spending 10 minutes on a technique or warm-up exercises, working on a lesson or two from this book for 20 minutes, and practicing a song for 15 minutes. Some examples for weekly goals might include working on four to five lessons from this book, practicing a song that you like, and spending 10 minutes a day on technique-improving exercises for your guitar playing. It should also be said that your weekly goals should not be too rigid (for example, "I *must* learn all of *Layla* this week.") or extremely lofty (for example, "This week, I'm going to learn 20 Foo Fighters' songs.").

Although letting your unconscious mind roam freely as you strum the guitar and noodle around with riffs and licks on the instrument is one important element to learning, discovery and improvement in music, try to keep this aspect of your playing to about 25% of your practicing. Sadly, many guitarists spend way too much time noodling around with their favorite sections of songs, ones that they are very comfortable playing. This often leads to guitarists falling into ruts with their playing (staying at the same level without improving). Though it is a lot of fun to noodle around on the guitar and play little riffs and licks, it's very important to be focused about your practicing and set clear goals for about 75% of your work time.

So, let's get started: Your lesson for today is to find a notebook or looseleaf binder that will be your practice journal. It does not have to be anything fancy or expensive. Take a few moments now to find one. If you do not have one around the house, buy one for a few dollars at a local store or online. This little investment will yield very positive results. Now, on the first page of the journal, write today's date, a lesson or two from this book that you would like to work on, and how much time you plan on spending on your guitar practice. You should continue this process for each day you practice. Some people like to cross off each task as they complete it. As well, it's often a good idea to write your next day's practice schedule at the end of your current day's practice session. This way, at some level, your mind will already be thinking about and planning for the next day's work; it's a good way to build and sustain momentum.

Good News! This edition includes free, bonus lessons. Go to the Home Page of SteeplechaseMusic.com. At the top of the Home Page, you will see a link for Guitar Books. Follow the link to the Guitar Books webpage. Then, click on the link for *The Guitar Scales Handbook*. On the webpage for the book, click Bonus Lessons and download the PDF and MP3 Audio Files

Have Fun!

Lesson #14: Electronic Tuners

One idea that you may add to your guitar playing is using an electronic tuner.

There are several benefits to having a portable tuner. First off, you can tune the guitar quickly with a great deal of accuracy. You can also check your guitar's tuning after playing a few songs (during a practice session, band rehearsal, or performance). Next, you can tune the guitar accurately without access to a piano, keyboard, pitch pipe, tuning fork, or fixed-pitch tuning instrument or device.

These tuners come in all sorts of shapes and sizes. The most popular and practical are clip-on tuners (in the illustration at the bottom to the left) and guitar-tuner apps (in the upper and bottom right illustrations). They range in prices from free (for many of the Apps that will work on smartphones, tablets, and computers) to around $20. You can find them online or at your local music store.

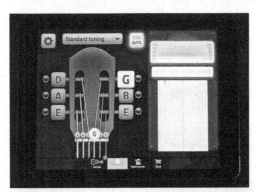

Here are some examples of commonly used digital tuning devices and apps.

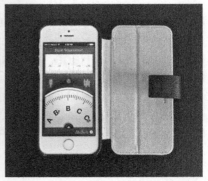

Lesson #15: Introduction to the Major Scale

Now we are going to learn our first scale: the C Major scale. This scale is the most common scale in music. It is used in thousands of songs and pieces, ranging from Pop to Rock to Classical to Country to Jazz. C is the root note of the C Major scale. A root note is the first note of the scale. The root note or most important note of the scale. We call most scales by their root notes, for example, C Major, A Major, D Minor, C# Minor, F Dorian Mode, etc.

All Major scales have a set pattern of whole steps and half steps. (Feel free to look back at lesson #1, to refresh your memory about half steps and whole steps.) "W" stands for whole step. "H" stands for half step. The pattern of steps for all Major scales is W, W, H, W, W, H.

Take a look at the forms for the C Major Scale below.

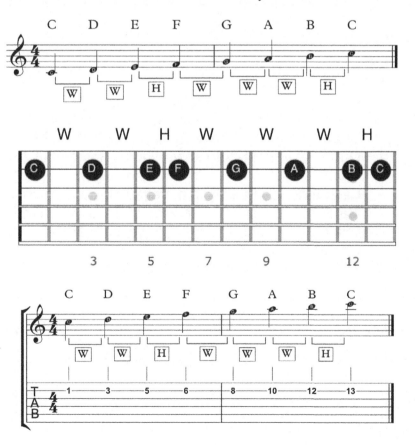

Lesson #16: C Major Scale, Part 1

In this lesson, we are going to learn the first four notes of the C Major scale going up (ascending) and going down (descending). The note names are written above the staff and inside the note heads. There is also indications for the fret and string numbers in the tablature (TAB).

This easy form of the C Major scale uses open strings. For example, to play the note D, you will pluck the fourth string open; your left hand will not fret any notes. The scale starts on the fifth string (the A string).

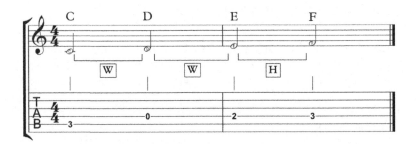

Check Out Video Lesson 3 Major Scale Basics

We are now going to look at the descending (going down) part of this four-note scale figure. Remember to curve your left-hand fingers so that you play the fretted notes with the tips of your fingers. Take your time and try to use your hearing and sense of touch, rather than your eyesight to coordinate the hands.

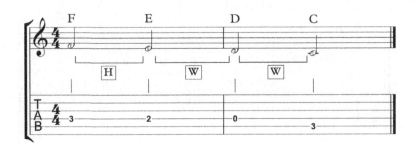

Lesson #17: C Major Scale, Part 2 & Kinesthetics for Guitar Playing

In this lesson, we are going to add the next four notes of the one-octave C Major scale.

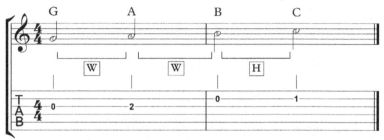

In the previous page, we discussed using your ears and sense of touch, rather than your eyes to coordinate your playing. Throughout the book, we will be developing and (hopefully) improving this skill. The awareness of the body's parts, their position, and their motion through space is called kinesthesia. It's something that we all use when driving, kicking or dribbling a ball, and walking up or down stairs, for example. Throughout your studies in this book, try to actively cultivate and improve your kinesthetic sense of the guitar: the position of your left hand on the fretboard and right hand on the strings. Ask yourself how does this hand position feel. Then, try to remember the feeling in your body, even if you are away from your guitar.

Now, we are going to practice the scale figure going down (descending).

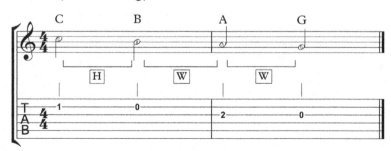

Lesson #18: C Major Scale, Part 3:
Putting It All Together

Great job! We are now ready to put the scale all together. Let's start by practicing the ascending pattern.

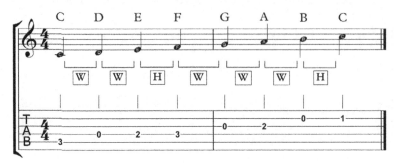

Now, let's practice the descending pattern. As best as you can, try to integrate your kinesthetic awareness while practicing. As an extra step, say (or sing on pitch) the notes of the scale as you are playing them. If you are shy about this, do it mentally. This will help make many different and important music-related neural connections for you.

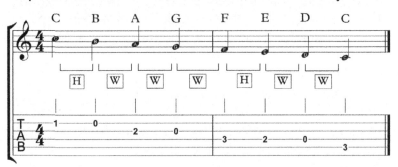

Let's work on the ascending and descending scale using the technique mentioned above on this page.

Lesson #19: C Major Scale Licks

Here are three open-string licks in C Major. You could use them in solos or fills over C Major, C7, and C Major 7 chords.

The first one has a Country or Bluegrass feel.

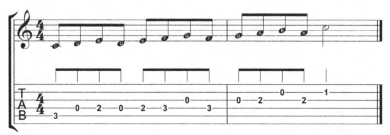

This next lick is inspired by fiddle playing and could be used as an intro, fill, or ending of a song, solo, or section of music. Feel free to draw your musical inspiration from other instruments and styles

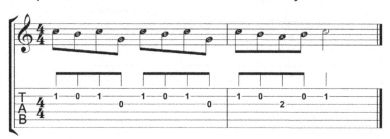

This open-string lick has repeated Gs for the fourth and fifth notes. Once you learn the lick, try varying it a little by repeating other notes in the phrase. With all of the licks in this book, once you learn them, explore variations on them using different techniques.

Lesson #20: More C Major Scale Licks

Here are three more licks that can be used in C Major contexts. Now that you are getting a little bit used to play scale-based licks, focus on your alternate picking and try to play accurately. You might think about how much of your guitar pick is needed to pluck a string. Depending on your guitar, pick, and string gauge, this may vary quite a bit. You might be surprise at how little surface area on the pick and string you need to activate to make a full sound. Once you start playing faster you will be using the minimum amount of motion to get the best musical result. Why not start to think about this now? In other words what could you do in your alternate picking technique to make your picking more efficient?

Here are three more lick in C Major to practice:

Lesson #21: Guitar Technique: Slides

Slides are a great technique to add nuance and new colors to your guitar playing. Sliding is a very popular guitar technique and is relatively easy to master. Basically, it just entails sliding one of your left-hand fingers up or down the fretboard between notes. This glissando effect will give your playing a vocal quality, like a great Rock or Blues singer.

You may hear a little buzzing or squeaking sound from the strings as you are sliding up or down. This is completely normal and is often part of the effect of the technique. Later on in the book and videos, you will learn about vibrato technique. When you combine slides and vibrato, your

Check Out Video Lesson 4: Guitar Technique: Slides

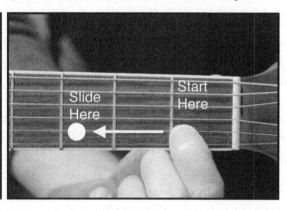

This is the basic technique for playing slides on the guitar: First, fret a note, pluck the string, then slide your left-hand finger to another fret (up or down) on the same string, without picking the string again. Try to let the notes ring out as you slide up or down the string. For a small slide, you can just go up or down one fret. Give this a try. For a bigger slide, try plucking a note and sliding your finger five or six frets up or down. Do you hear the difference in sound? Now, try sliding up to a new note and then slide back to the original fret.

Also, as you are sliding, only press down on the string as much as is needed to keep the note ringing. If you press down too hard, it will hurt your finger and make it difficult to slide up and down the fretboard.

Lesson #22: Slide Licks

Below, is a slide lick. On the High-E string (the 1st string), slide up from the 1st fret to the 3rd fret. Then, slide down from the 3rd fret to the 1st fret. Listen to the effect. Try playing it slowly a few times. Slide to the notes in a leisurely manner. Once you have that down, try sliding into the notes quickly.

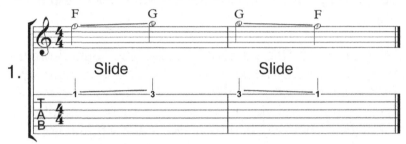

Try these two guitar licks that use slides. In the first one, you will slide between the 3rd and 5th frets on the 2nd string (the B string) and also play the open High-E string. The second example is on the 1st string. It combines the sounds of slides and open strings. As you learn these guitar licks, and all of the licks in this book, experiment with the sound of each lick (change the speed of your playing, add a few notes here and there, etc.). A big part of becoming a good guitar player is articulating each note in a meaningful way. So, have fun discovering new ways to play each one of the guitar licks.

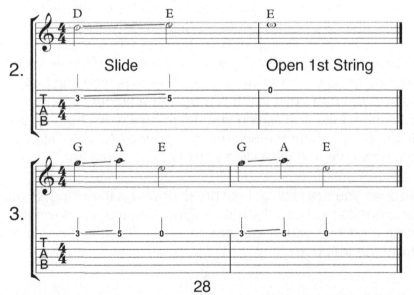

28

Lesson #23: Music Theory Overview: What are Intervals?

Intervals are the distances between any two notes. On the guitar, intervals can move horizontally (along the neck on one string) or vertically (up or down from one string to another). **Check Out Video Lesson 5: On Intervals.**

Intervals give scales, melodies, and chords their distinctive characteristics. They are the building blocks of them. Below, you will see a chart with the basic intervals and their names laid out on the High E string of the guitar: going from F on the first fret to F on the thirteenth fret (one octave total). Take a moment and play F to Gb. This is a minor second interval. Now, play F to G. This is a major second interval. Play F to Ab. This is a minor third interval. Repeat this process from going all the way from F on the first fret to F on the thirteenth fret. As you are playing, listen to the distinctive quality of each interval. For example, the minor seconds played back and forth might sound like the *Jaws* theme. *Have fun!*

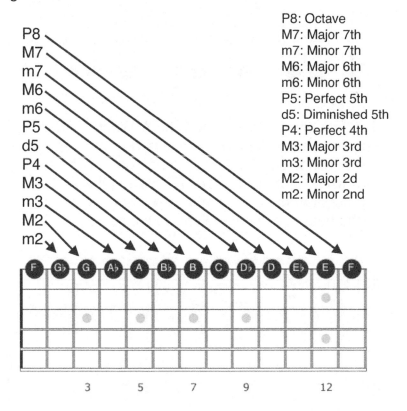

P8: Octave
M7: Major 7th
m7: Minor 7th
M6: Major 6th
m6: Minor 6th
P5: Perfect 5th
d5: Diminished 5th
P4: Perfect 4th
M3: Major 3rd
m3: Minor 3rd
M2: Major 2d
m2: Minor 2nd

Lesson #24: Introduction to the Minor Scale

The most prominent characteristic of the Minor scale is the Minor 3rd between the A and C notes. (See chart below.) This Minor 3rd interval gives the A Minor scale its most distinctive characteristic. To hear this, play the open A on the fifth string and then play the C on the third fret of the fifth string. Listen to the interval. Play A to C a few times. Then play C to A a few times.

> Check Out Video Lesson 6: Minor Scale Basics

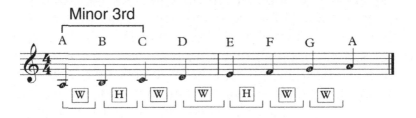

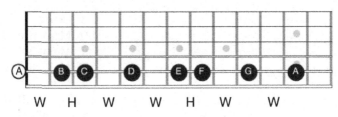

The first chart above shows the A Minor scale in one octave. The middle chart shows a neck diagram of the A Minor scale on one string with the half steps and whole steps indicated. Try playing the scale from the diagram on the A string (fifth string). The diagram at the bottom of the page shows the scale with TAB.

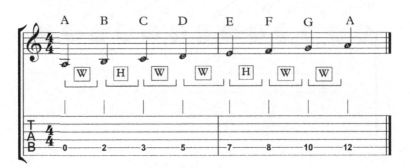

Lesson #25: A Minor Scale, Part 1

In this lesson, we are going to play through the first four notes of the A Minor scale. This easy version of the scale uses a number of open strings on the guitar, for example, the open A string (fifth string) and the open D string (fourth string).

All Minor scales have a related Major scale. This means that for every Major scale there is a corresponding Minor scale that has the same notes, but in a slightly different order. The A Minor scale is the relative Minor scale for C Major. They both share the same notes. Here are the notes for the C Major scale (in order from lower to higher): C, D, E, F, G, A, B, C. Here are the notes for A Minor scale (in order from lower to higher): A, B, C, D, E, F, G, A. You might notice that the A Minor scale starts on the sixth note of the C Major scale and proceeds in the same order from that point. All Minor scales are based on the sixth degree of their relative Major scale.

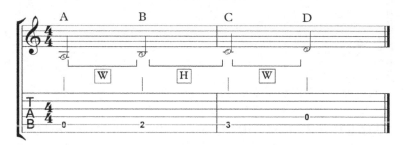

The ascending A Minor scale (first four notes) is in the diagram above; the descending version is below.

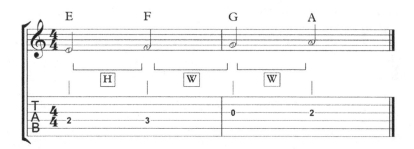

Lesson #26: A Minor Scale, Part 2

In this lesson, we are going to work on the 4 remaining notes of the one-octave A Minor scale: E, F, G, and A.

There is an alternate name for the Minor scale, by the way. The name is the Aeolian Mode. Later in the book, we are going to learn these Modes of the Major scale. However, if you come across (or have come across) the term "Aeolian Mode", just know that is another way of naming the Minor scale.

In the first exercise in this lesson, we are going to practice ascending (going up) the second half of the A Minor scale. You might notice that the G note is played by the open third string on the guitar.

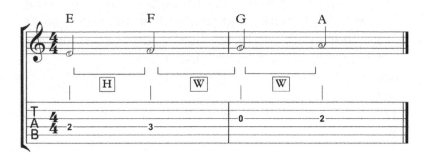

In the second exercise in this lesson, we are going to play the retrograde (reverse) of the musical figure from the first exercise. We will play a descending figure, going from the A down to the E. Take your time with the exercises on this page and don't move on to the next lesson until you feel comfortable with the exercises.

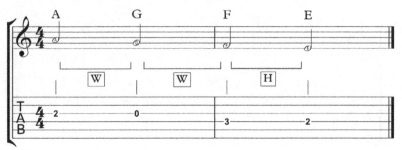

Lesson #27: A Minor Scale, Part 3:
Putting It All Together

Now, let's put together what we have learned in the previous two lessons. This first lesson exercise is for the one-octave A Minor scale ascending.

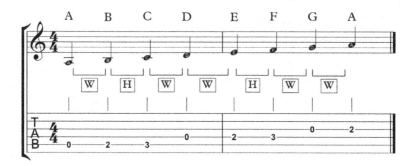

The second exercise is for the scale descending.

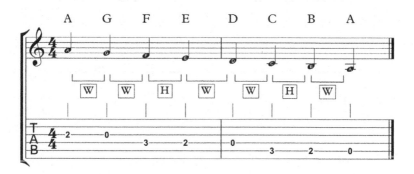

In the third exercise, let's play the ascending and then descending one-octave A Minor Scale.

Lesson #28: A Minor Scale Licks

Here are three licks in A Minor. You can play them A Minor chords or chords progressions in the key of A Minor. The first lick is a nod to the great violinist / composer Paganini who has inspired shredder guitarists from Yngwie Malmsteen to Steve Vai.

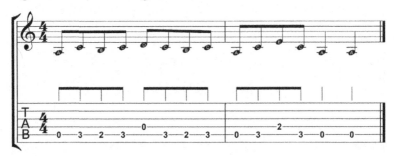

This second lick in A Minor is also a neoclassical guitar idea that uses opens strings.

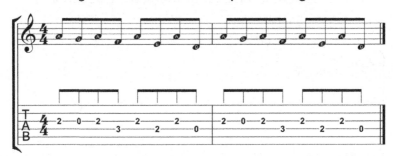

The final lick on this page starts with notes of the A Minor arpeggio. (An arpeggio is a chord played one note at a time, rather than the notes played all at once.) This A Minor arpeggio starts on the third of the chord.

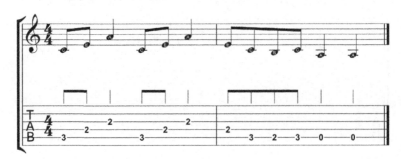

Lesson #29: Vibrato Technique

Vibrato is one of the most expressive techniques in guitar playing. The technique, which involves slightly moving the guitar string up and down or side to side, will give the sound of the notes you play a shimmering, vocal quality. When you add vibrato to your playing, you will emulate the techniques of Rock, Blues, and Jazz singers on your guitar. This will make the musical phrases that you play sound more expressive and dramatic.

We will be looking at two types of vibrato: Wide Vibrato and Close Vibrato. To learn more, check out the video lesson.

> # Check Out Video Lesson 7:
> # Guitar Technique: Vibrato

To create a wide, dramatic vibrato, place the left-hand third finger on a fret (let's try the 3rd fret of the B string) and move your finger in an up-and-down motion, after plucking the B string. Listen to sound quality. If you need more support for your third finger, you might want to place your first and second fingers on the first and second frets of the B string, respectively. This will provide greater leverage on the string. Once you have this technique down, try to vary the speed of your up-and-down movements. The faster your vibrato, the more energy and wildness will be in the sound.

For a more subtle vibrato, fret a note with your left hand and wiggle your finger back and forth after plucking the string. This is a great sounding vibrato for ballads and slow songs. Listen to Eric Clapton and Jimi Hendrix for vibrato styles.

On the following page, there are some illustrations of these two different types of vibrato techniques. Take your time to explore the nearly infinite variety of sounds that you can generate from slightly different types of vibrato. *Have fun!*

For a more intense vibrato, wiggle your finger up and down, while pressing down on the string.

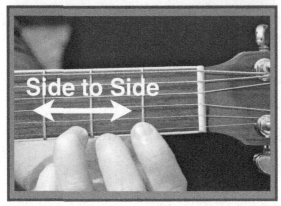

For a more subtle vibrato, wiggle your finger side to side, while pressing down on the string.

Lesson #30: Vibrato Licks in C Major & A Minor

Try these two vibrato licks: in C Major & A Minor.

This is the symbol for vibrato.

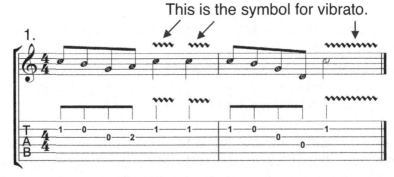

36

Lesson #31: Music Theory: A Review of Intervals

"Intervals" are the distances between two notes in music. For example, the distance between the notes "E" and "F" on your fretboard (the open E string and the 1st fret of the E string) is an interval, which is called a "minor second".

Here are some common names for intervals: minor second, major third, minor third, perfect 4th, perfect 5th, and octave. While these names may seem a bit technical, they just indicate the space between 2 notes. Try playing the intervals listed in the chart below on the high E string and listen to the difference in sounds. Intervals are what gives each scale its unique sound: for example, why major scales sound different than minor scales.

> ## Intervals on the 1st String

1. Open String then 1st Fret = Minor 2nd

2. Open String then 2nd Fret = Major 2nd

3. Open String then 3rd Fret = Minor 3rd

4. Open String then 4th Fret = Major 3rd

5. Open String then 5th Fret = Perfect 4th

6. Open String then 6th Fret = Diminished 5th

7. Open String then 7th Fret = Perfect 5th

8. Open String then 8th Fret = Minor 6th

9. Open String then 9th Fret = Major 6th

10. Open String then 10 Fret = Minor 7th

11. Open String then 11th Fret = Major 7th

12. Open String then 12th Fret = Octave

On the guitar, intervals can go horizontally (like the example above) or vertically (going up or down from one string to another string). We go over intervals in a lot more detail in the *Ultimate Guitar Chords, Scales, Arpeggios Handbook* by Damon Ferrante.

Lesson #32: Minor Pentatonic Warm-up Exercises

On the next few pages, we are going to look at the A Minor Pentatonic. In preparation for this scale and its modes, we are going to practice two-note-per-string patterns. Take your time to master these patterns before moving on to the actual Minor Pentatonic scales.

By the way, "modes" are just the scale pattern starting on a different bottom (or "root" note - to use the musical term). For example, if the notes of a scale are A, C, D, E, and G, a mode would be C, D, E, G, A: the same pattern of notes, starting on C instead of A.

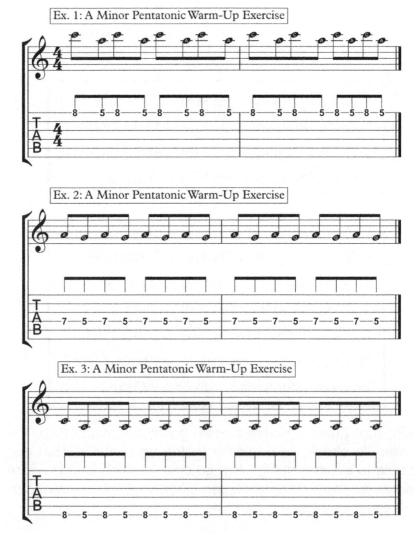

Ex. 1: A Minor Pentatonic Warm-Up Exercise

Ex. 2: A Minor Pentatonic Warm-Up Exercise

Ex. 3: A Minor Pentatonic Warm-Up Exercise

Lesson #33: Technique-Building Exercises

Here are three more technique-building exercises that we will focus on in our preparation for learning the A Minor Pentatonic Scale. These three exercises emphasize patterns on two adjacent strings.

With each of the exercises on this page (as well as for all of the scales, licks, and exercises in this book and on the video lessons) please start slowly and gradually build up your speed.

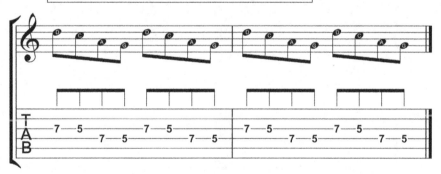

Ex. 1: A Minor Pentatonic Warm-Up Exercise

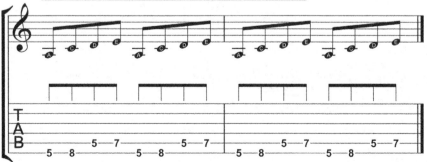

Ex. 2: A Minor Pentatonic Warm-Up Exercise

Ex. 3: A Minor Pentatonic Warm-Up Exercise

Lesson #34: A Minor Pentatonic Overview

Pentatonic Minor is a Five-Note Scale. In the key of A, the notes are A, C, D, E, and G. The Pentatonic Minor is closely related to the "Blues Scale" and is used in Rock, Jazz, Pop, Country, and Blues songs.

There are 5 Modes of the Pentatonic Minor Scale. These Modes start on a different note of the Pentatonic Minor Scale and ascend ("go up") the scale, following its pattern of steps. For example, the notes of Mode 1 are A, C, D, E, and G; the notes of Mode 2 are C, D, E, G, and A. As you can see, Mode 2 has the same notes as Mode 1, but in a different order

Here are the note and the fingering patterns for the A Minor Pentatonic Scale. Practice playing this pattern ascending and descending (going up and down) until you have memorized the fingering. This is one of the most commonly used scales in many styles of music.

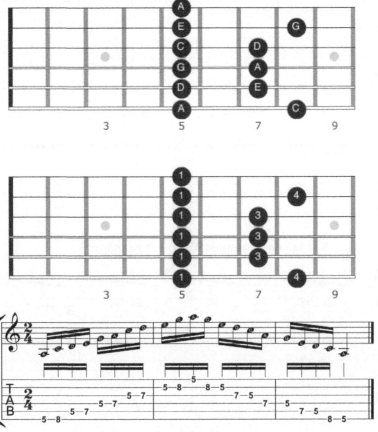

40

Lesson #35: Pentatonic Minor Licks

In this lesson, we are going to work on some licks that use the Pentatonic Minor scale in the key of A. These licks can be used over Blues, Rock, Country, and many other styles, when playing in the key of A. Also, once you learn them, feel free to move the licks around the guitar neck to play in other keys.

Try out these three licks. They can all be played using an A Pentatonic Minor Scale. The first one uses sequences: repeating patterns of notes. The second and third examples use triplets.

Also, if you haven't done so already, take a minute to download the free bonus lessons (in PDF and MP3 Audio format). The bonus lessons cover 100 licks that you can use in your playing. Go to the *Guitar Scales Handbook* webpage on steeplechasemusic.com and follow the links to the bonus lessons.

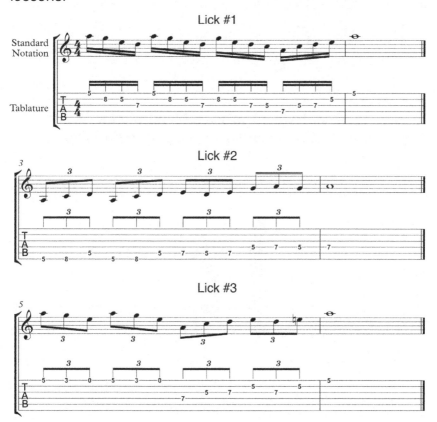

Lesson #36: Moveable Scales:
G Minor & B Pentatonic Minor Scales

The scales that we will be learning for the rest of the book are called "moveable scales". In other words, you can use one pattern, like the pattern for the A Pentatonic Minor scale, in all other keys, Like G, F, Bb, C#, etc. All you need to do is start the pattern on the root note of the scale.

For example, to play the G Minor Pentatonic scale in Mode 1, just put your index finger on the 3rd fret of the 6th string (the Low E) and play the same finger pattern that you learned for the A Minor Pentatonic two pages ago.

Here is the scale chart:

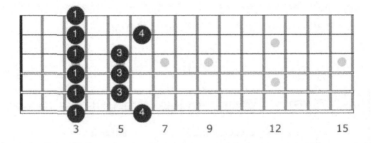

To play the Minor Pentatonic scale Mode 1 in the key of B, just move the pattern that you just played (from the chart above) to the 7th fret of the 6th string.

Here is the scale chart:

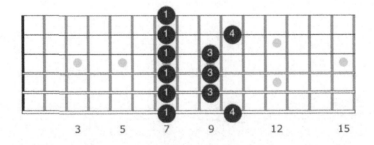

These two scales should sound both similar and different: the same pattern, but different notes.

Lesson #37: A Pentatonic Minor: Mode 2

Let's now look at Mode 2 of the A Pentatonic Minor scale. Mode 2 uses the same notes of the Pentatonic Minor scale; however, it starts on the second note of the scale.

The notes of the A Minor Pentatonic scale Mode 1 are: A, C, D, E, G.

The notes of the A Minor Pentatonic scale Mode 2 are: C, D, E, G, A.

Do you notice how the same collection of notes are used, but in a slightly different order? This reordering of the notes gives each mode its particular sound color.

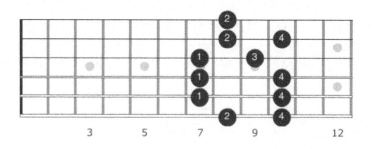

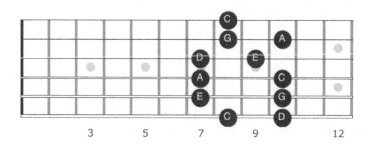

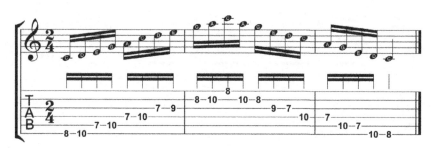

Lesson #38: Pentatonic Minor Mode 2 Licks

In this lesson, we are going play some classic Blues licks, based on Mode 2 of the A Minor Pentatonic scale, that can be used over A7 or A Minor 7 chords.

The first one covers an octave from C to C.

This second lick could be used as a fill or to end a phrase or song, especially a Blues or Minor Blues in A. It wiggles up to a high C. Have some fun exploring the speed and style of your vibrato at the end of the phrase.

The third lick in this lesson is in the lower register of the guitar. It starts and ends on the C of the sixth string on the guitar. Also, try exploring the vibrato at the end.

Lesson #39: Guitar Technique: String Bending

Bending the strings is a great technique to add expressiveness to your lead guitar playing. Basically, you will push the string up far enough to get the pitch to change (to go higher). This takes a good deal of effort. So, the key is to use three of your fingers to bend the string, instead of just the finger on the fret you're trying to bend. You can accomplish this by placing your third finger on the fret you're trying to bend. Place your first and second fingers on the frets behind it, and exert power with all three fingers pushing upward and down on the string. It's easiest to bend notes on the 2nd string.

Check Out Video Lesson 8: String Bends

Half-Step Bend: On the second string, place your index finger on the 6th fret, middle finger on the 7th fret, and ring finger on the 8th fret. Use the strength of all 3 fingers to bend (push) the note on the 8th fret up a half step.

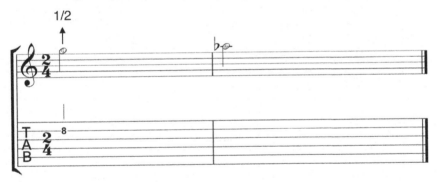

Whole-Step Bend: On the second string, place your index finger on the 6th fret, middle finger on the 7th fret, and ring finger on the 8th fret. Use the strength of all three fingers to bend (push) the note on the 8th fret up a whole step.

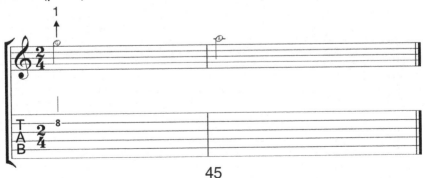

String-bend preparation and bend photos (above).

Check out Video Lesson 8

Lesson #40: String-Bending Licks with the A Minor Pentatonic Scale

Here are three string-bend licks in A Pentatonic Minor.

Lesson #41: Learning the Notes of the Fretboard: High E String: 1st String

Throughout the book, we are going to work on learning the notes on the guitar neck.

In this first chart of the neck, we are going to learn the notes of the High E string (first string).

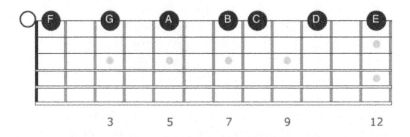

With your guitar in hand and using the above chart, locate the natural notes of the High E String.

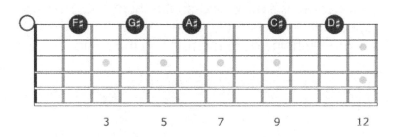

For the next two charts, locate first the sharp notes and then the flat notes on your guitar neck.
Now, close the book and quiz yourself on the notes.

Lesson #42: A Pentatonic Minor Mode 3

In this lesson, we are going to learn Mode 3 of the A Pentatonic Minor scale. In the first chart, you will find the notes of the scale. Take a moment to review these on your guitar.

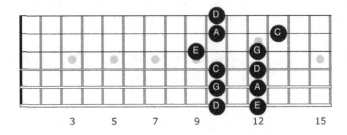

In the chart below, you can practice the fingerings for the scale. Remember to play with the tips of the fingers of your left hand. Play the scale two times in a row, going up and down. Then, take a break for about twenty to thirty seconds and relax your hands and arms and shake them out. Then, repeat the exercise five to ten more times. This will greatly help you in memorizing the scale.

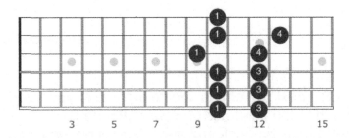

Below is the notation for the scale going up and down.

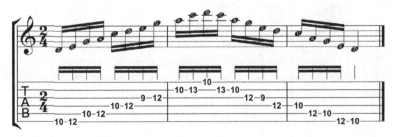

48

Lesson #43: A Pentatonic Minor Mode 4

Here is another very useful Mode of the Pentatonic Minor scale. Remember that all of the Modes and scales from this section onward are moveable. In other words, you can play them in any key simply by moving them to an appropriate starting note on the guitar neck. For, example, to transpose the Pentatonic Mode 4 to the key of D, just move your index finger down to the fifth fret of your guitar and play the same pattern listed below.

Here are the fingerings for Mode 4 in A.

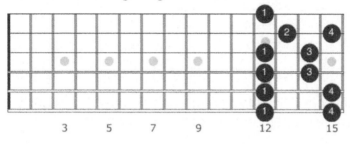

Here are the notes for Mode 4 in A.

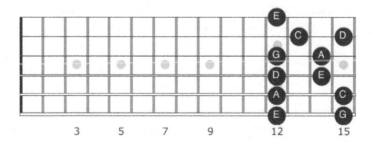

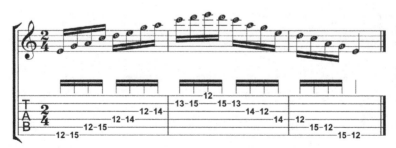

Lesson #44: Pentatonic Minor Licks for Modes 3 & 4

Here are three A Pentatonic Minor Licks that will get you into playing on higher frets of the guitar. Take your time with these, since they may be in a new finger position for you

The first lick is a good workout for fingers one and four. Try to play the notes for finger four on the tip of the finger.

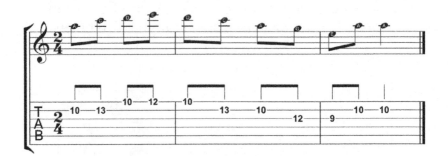

The second lick starts on a high G note. Try to bring your thumb a bit behind the neck to help with the reach.

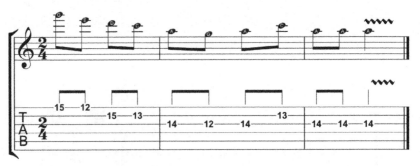

The last lick starts on the sixth string and is a good exercise for getting around on upper frets of the guitar.

Lesson #45: Tone and Volume Controls and Effects

A great way to vary your tone is to change the settings on the volume and tone knobs on your guitar. Most electric (and some acoustic) guitars have tone and volume controls. If you are playing an electric guitar, try lowering or raising the volume level by turning the volume knob. You might notice, as you do this, that the treble or bass in the guitar's signal goes up or down. You might also hear that the gain is increased or decreased.

If you are playing with distortion and a lead tone, try turning the volume knob down a few settings. For instance, try turning it from ten down to seven. You will hear the tone change and the sound will become a little cleaner, as well as a little less treble oriented.

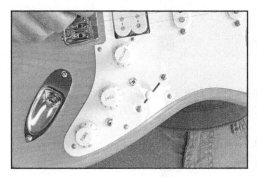 

The volume knob can also create volume-swell effects. Try this technique: turn the volume knob to zero, then strum a chord loudly and quickly turn the volume knob all the way up to ten. You will hear the sound fade in quickly. Try experimenting with the speed of the fade in. The tone knob can create wah-wah effects, in a similar way, when you pluck a note and turn the knob quickly from 0 to 10.

One good technique for controlling the volume and tone knobs is to use your right-hand pinky finger to roll the knob to the desired level or to create swells. (See photo) By using your pinky, you won't need to let go of the guitar pick. It's also a simpler motion than using your thumb and index finger; so you can do the swells much faster.

Lesson #46: A Pentatonic Minor Mode 5

In this lesson, we are going to learn Mode 5 of the A Minor Pentatonic scale. For ease of playing, we have moved this scale to the third fret of the Low-E String. However, it could also be played with the same fingering on the fifteenth fret.

This Mode form is a good exercise for developing coordination between fingers one and four and also for fingers two and four.

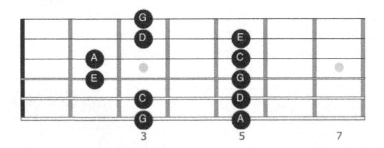

The notes are above and fingerings below.

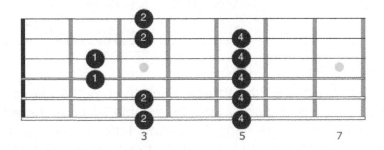

Lesson #47: Pentatonic Minor Mode 5 Licks

Here are three, Blues-influenced licks that use Mode 5 of the A Pentatonic Minor scale. In the first example, there is a lick that uses a repeating four-note figure to build up energy. Try picking the four-note groups in a slightly different manner each time you play them.

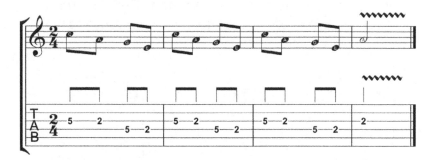

The second example in this lesson uses an ascending lick to travel from a low G up to an A note.

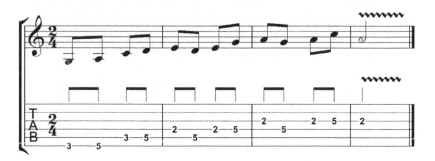

The third lick starts on a high G and travels down to A.

Lesson #48: Learning the Notes of the Fretboard: B String: 2nd String

In this lesson, we are going to learn the notes of the B string (the second string). Study each chart with your guitar in hand, naming the notes aloud as you play them. Try to memorize a few notes (maybe 3) at a time. Then, turn the book over and quiz yourself on the notes you have just studied. Return back to this memorization technique over a week and you will see progress.

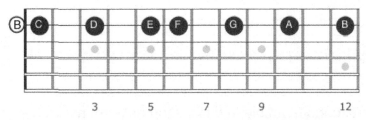

As you work on the chart above for the natural notes on the B string, try to visualize the chart in your mind. Imagine that you are holding your guitar and fretting the notes in the correct places along the guitar neck.

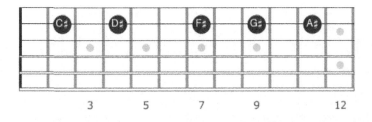

Above and below are the charts for the sharps and flats on the B string, respectively.

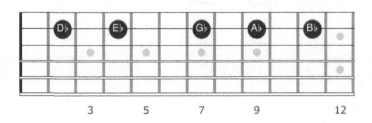

Lesson #49: Music Theory Overview:
What are Major Scales?

All Major Scales follow the same pattern that is composed of whole steps and half steps in a set order. You might remember that a half step on the guitar is the distance from one fret to the next on a single string, for example F to F# on the High E string. H = Half Step. See example below:

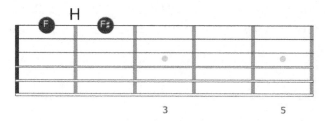

On the guitar, a whole step is twice the size of a half step: two half steps combined. An example of a whole step would be the distance from the notes F to G on the High E string. W = Whole Step. See example below.

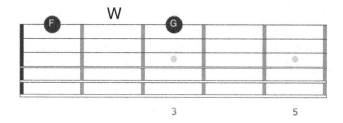

Here is the F Major Scale on one string with the whole steps (W) and half steps (H) indicated. Try playing it.

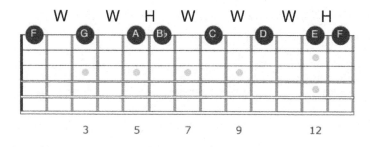

Lesson #50: Technique-Building Exercises: Major

On this page, let's practice the main three-note-per-string patterns that are used for the Major Scale and its modes in this book. Once you learn these patterns, move them up and down the neck. Also, play them on different strings.

The first pattern uses fingers one, two, and four. The second pattern uses fingers one, three, and four. The third pattern also uses fingers one, two, and four; however, you will skip a fret between fingers one and two. With all of these patterns, start slowly and gradually build up your speed and coordination.

Lesson #51:
Technique-Building Exercises, Part 2: Major

Let's continue with three more technique-building exercises for the Major Scale and its modes. In these three exercise, we are going to play two- and three-string patterns. If you haven't done so already, please **Check Out Video Lesson 9 on 3NPS Scales**. The video will give you additional information on alternate picking and demonstrate ways to hold your guitar pick that will improve your speed and accuracy.

If you have a metronome or a metronome app, it might be a good idea to start integrating its use in your scales practicing, as well.

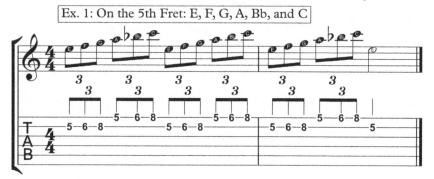

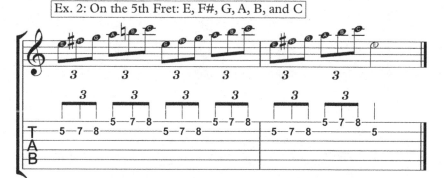

Lesson #52:
C Major Scale from the 5th String (3NPS)

The forms of the C Major Scale and its modes that we will be focusing on in this section are based on a three-note-per-string system. This system makes learning the hand patterns easy. It also makes it easier to play scale licks at high speed, since the right-hand picking is very regular.

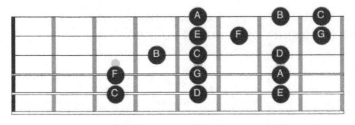

Above, is the note pattern for the scale. Below, you will find the finger pattern, the standard notation, and the tablature for the scale. Take your time and learn the pattern for each string. Then, gradually put it all together.

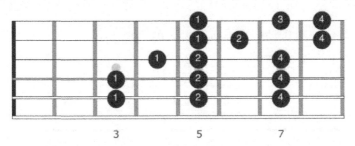

Later in the book, we are going to learn the Major Scale and Modes in the CAGED system. The scale forms from the CAGED system are also very useful. However, they have irregular fingerings, which makes them a little more complicated to learn and conceptualize.

Lesson #53: Licks with the C Major Scale

Here are three licks that use the C major scale. Each one uses open strings to help you change positions on the guitar neck quickly. After you learn them, take a little time to explore making variations on each lick. You might reverse the order of some of the notes or add slides, bends, and vibrato.

Throughout this book, the licks presented are just a starting point. Feel free to modify them to suit your playing. You might consider them as an initial example for your explorations of the melodic possibilities for each scale. There are infinite variations for expression and a lifetime's worth of musical discovery.

Have Fun!

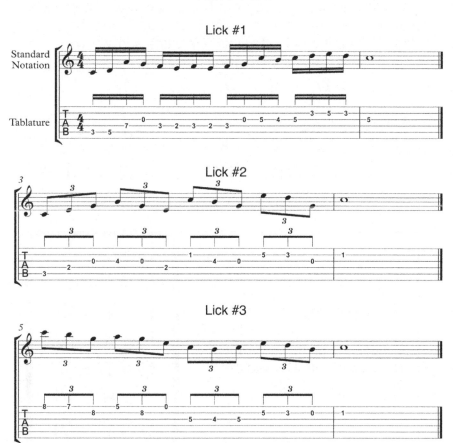

Lesson #54: Music Theory Overview: What are Root Notes and Scale Degrees?

In all major and minor scales, we give the notes numbers based on their position. These numbers go from one to seven. In music, we call these numbers "scale degrees". The numbers are often written as Roman Numerals (see chartS below).

The root (the main note of the scale) is always number (or degree) one. In the key of C, the notes are C, D, E, F, G, A, and B. Each one of these notes is given a number from 1 to 7. Basically, the numbers just start from the root note, which is number one, and go up in order to seven. So, it's pretty simple and doesn't require any advanced math skills. Take a moment and slowly play through the Major scale from two pages ago. As you are playing the scale, say the letter name and then the scale degree for each note. Try this a few times in a row.

Here are the Notes and Corresponding Numbers for the Scale Degrees in the Key of C Major. The Roman Numerals for Each Scale Degree are written on the Right.	C = 1 = I D = 2 = II E = 3 = III F = 4 = IV G = 5 = V A = 6 = VI B = 7 = VII

Lesson #55: What are chord progressions?

A chord progression is just a fancy term that means a group of chords that follows a particular pattern. These patterns often repeat several times during a song. In Rock, Blues, Country, Metal, Folk, and Pop there are several chord progressions that are very common. You have probably heard these progressions hundreds of times.

Chord progressions are given names based on the scale degree numbers of the root notes of the chords. For instance, a chord progression in C Major that features only the chords C, F, and G is called a I, IV, V progression — pronounced like this: "a one, four, five progression". Refer to the chart below for the scale degrees.

Below is a graphic representation of the scale degrees in C Major. The scale degrees are written as Roman Numerals at the bottom of the diagram.

Letter Names:

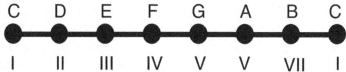

Scale Degrees:

Below is a I, V, IV, V, I chord progression. Take a minute to play these notes. Have you heard a similar chord progression in any songs?

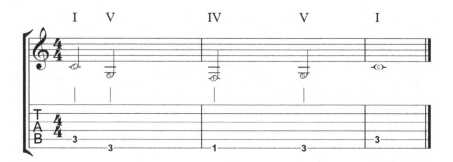

Lesson #56: What are the Modes?

There are 7 Modes of the Major Scale. Each Mode begins on one of the notes of the Major Scale. For example, the Dorian Mode begins on the second note of the C Major scale: the note D. In the example below, we have the C Major scale (above) and the Dorian Mode (below). They use the same notes, just in a different order.

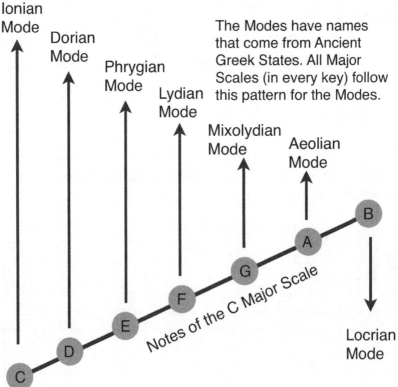

The Modes have names that come from Ancient Greek States. All Major Scales (in every key) follow this pattern for the Modes.

Lesson #57: Music Theory Overview:
What are "Mode Groups"

A lot of musicians group the modes into two or three basic groups, based on the harmonies and/or chords with which they predominantly interweave.

The first group is composed of scales that are oriented toward Major chords. Major chords are chords that have a Major 3rd interval between the root and the 3rd of the chord. (If you would like to learn a lot more about chords, check out the *Ultimate Guitar Chords, Scales & Arpeggios Handbook*, also by Damon Ferrante.) The modes that fit into this set are the Major scale (also know as the Ionian Mode), the Lydian Mode (based on scale degree IV), and the Mixolydian Mode (based on scale degree V). Each of these modes has a characteristic sound, which we will go into in more detail in the following pages. However, they all work well over Major chords. Quite often, depending on the musical context of a song or piece, you might be able to interchange them, depending on the musical idea that you would like to express.

The second group is composed of scales that are oriented toward Minor chords. Minor chords are chords that have a Minor 3rd interval between the root and the 3rd of the chord. The modes that fit into this set are the Dorian Mode (based on scale degree II), the Phygian Mode (based on scale degree III), and the Aeolian Mode (also know as the Minor scale, based on scale degree VI). Each of these modes also has its own character.

The last group, depending on one's school of thought, are scales that are oriented toward Dominant chords: Major chords with an added dominant 7th interval above the root. The Mixolydian Mode falls into this category.

Lastly, you may have noticed that we left out the Locrian Mode (based on scale degree VII). We will get to that one a little later in the book.

Lesson #58: Dorian Mode from the 5th String: Three Notes Per String (3NPS)

The Dorian Mode is a Minor tonality mode. It is great to use over Minor chords. It has been used in a wide variety of contexts from modal Jazz (like Miles Davis) to Classic Rock (like the Beatles and Led Zeppelin). It can give a lighter Minor feel to songs and guitar solos.

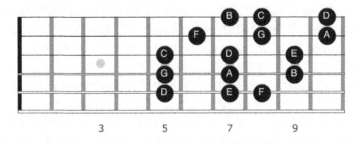

The main difference between the Dorian Mode and the Minor scale is the sixth degree.

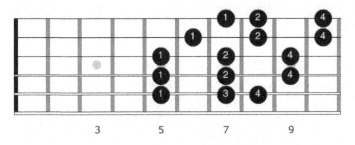

In the Minor scale the sixth degree is flat. In this case it would be a Bb rather than a B natural.

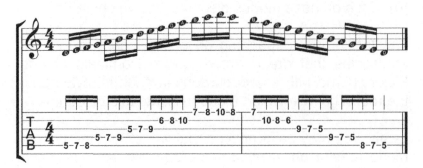

64

Lesson #59: Dorian Mode Licks

The Dorian Mode is a minor scale that has a folk-like character (think *Greensleeves*). It shares the same collection of notes as the C Major Scale, but it goes from D to D.

These three licks could be used over a chord progression in D Minor, where you would like to give a slightly different character to the minor sound, one that might evoke Renaissance music, for example.

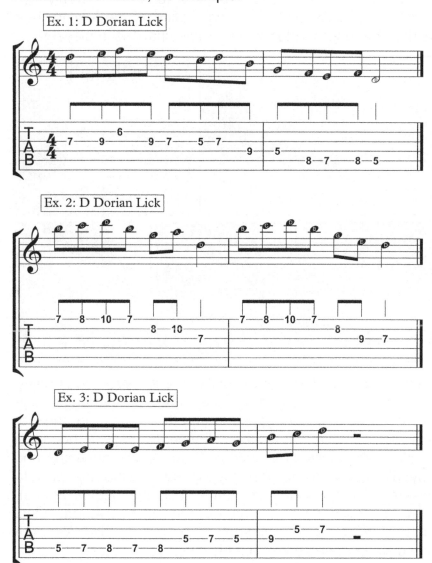

Lesson #60:
Getting Different Tones from Your Guitar

The angle and placement of your guitar pick:

By changing the angle, speed, and power of your picking motion in the right hand, you can greatly vary the tone of your guitar playing. The guitar pick is the point at which you come into contact with the strings. So, slight variations in the motion and angle will alter the guitar tone considerably. For most great players, the picking motion is the key to their sound. Have fun exploring these little changes in playing!

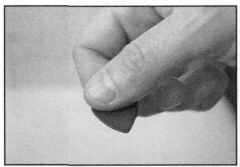

Stevie Ray Vaughan, for example, had a very strong picking technique, where he attacked the strings with an aggressive motion. Eric Johnson, although he often varies the angle of his pick for different sounds, frequently uses a bouncing motion when picking to create an articulate, punching and round tone. In your own playing try moving the pick to different locations on the strings (see the photos above). Also, try plucking with the back of the pick or different sides. You will notice a great change in the tone quality. Also, put the pick down sometimes and just use your fingers.

Lesson #61: Phrygian Mode from the 5th String: Three Notes Per String (3NPS)

The Phrygian Mode is a based on the third degree of the Major scale. It is a Minor scale that is very similar to the Aeolian Mode (also known as the Minor Scale). The only difference is that this scale has a flat two. For example the E Phrygian has an F natural as its second note; the E Aeolian has an F sharp as its second note. This flat two of the Phrygian gives the scale an exotic, dark quality.

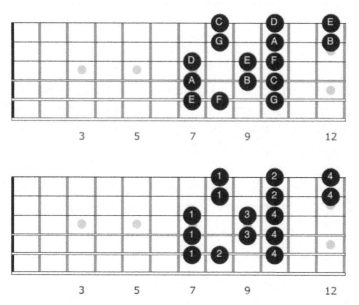

Above are the notes and fingerings for the E Phrygian scale. Below, you will find the tablature and standard notation for the scale.

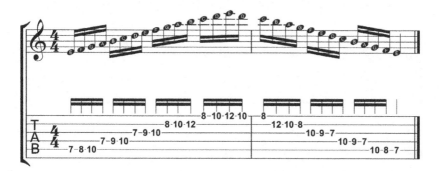

Lesson #62: Phrygian Mode Licks

Here are three Phrygian licks that can be used over E Minor chords. The first one plays on the sound created by the flat 2 of the scale (the note F). It outlines an E Minor 7 arpeggio and gives it an extra flourish with the addition of the flat 2 sound.

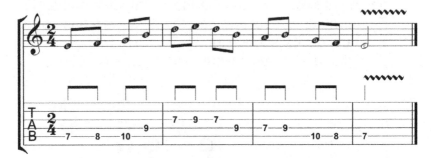

The second lick could be used in a song to build up the energy of a section. It features an E pedal point, a technique used in Baroque music and also in Neoclassical guitar styles.

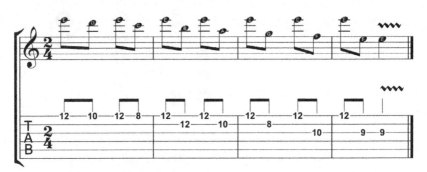

The third lick wends its way up an octave from E to E giving an exotic turn to a Minor sound.

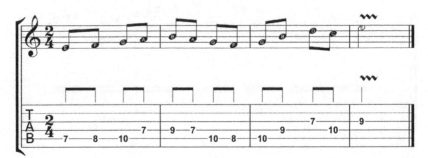

Lesson #63: Learning the Notes of the Fretboard: The 3rd String: G

You are making a lot of progress with learning the notes the guitar neck! This is such an essential skill for any guitarist. It will help you make steady progress and give you confidence in your playing. Knowing the notes of the neck will also make it much easier to communicate with musicians who play other instruments. For example, you will be able to say to a trumpet player, "I'm playing a G, A, and B." Rather than saying something like, "I'm not sure what the

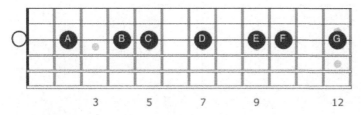

notes are. I'm playing the ones on the 3rd, 5th, and 7th frets of the High E string." Most non-guitarists wouldn't be able to translate that to their instruments.

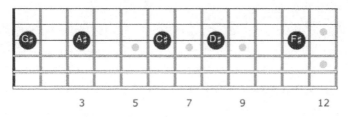

Follow the same techniques that you have been using for the other strings to learn the notes of the third string of the guitar (the G).

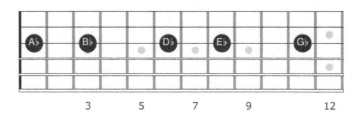

Lesson #64: Guitar Techniques: Pull Offs

Pull offs are a guitar technique where you fret a note and pull your finger down and off of the string without plucking the second note. You can pull off to another fretted note, for example, from the third finger to the first finger, or you can pull off from a fretted note to an open string. The technique should probably be called "pull downs", because that is a closer description of the motion. It is important that you use the tip of your finger when doing a pull off. This will give a more precise tone and make the technique easier to execute. Check out the video.

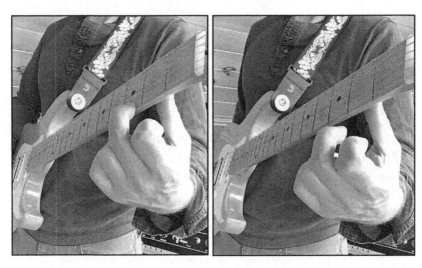

Check Out Video Lesson 10: Pull Offs

Try playing these pull offs on the High E string. Pull slightly downward. The "p" in the tablature stands for pull off.

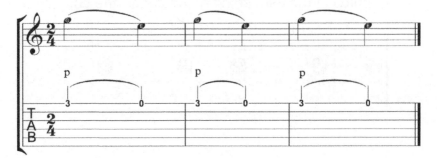

Lesson #65: Pull Off Licks

Here are three pull-off licks that you can use over E Minor chords or songs in E Minor. The first one is on the High E and B strings and has a slide near the end.

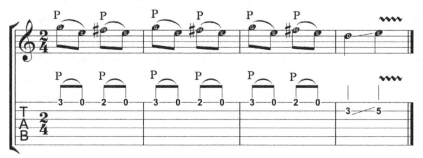

This second one is also on the High E string, primarily. Once you get the pattern in your hands try to speed it up a bit. Also, experiment with adding other notes in E Minor.

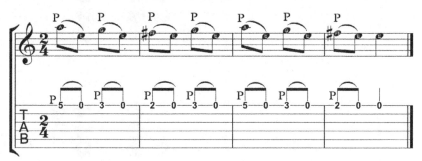

This last one is a fun lick that uses fretted E notes (on the 5th fret of the second string) and open E notes (the High E string). Even though the pitches are the same, the notes sound a bit different. It's good for a Minor Bluegrass song.

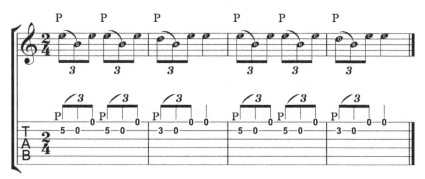

Lesson #66: Lydian Mode from the 5th String: Three Notes Per String (3NPS)

The Lydian Mode is based on the fourth degree of the Major scale. In terms of tonalities, the Lydian works very well over Major chords. The one essential difference between the Lydian Mode and the Major scale is that the Lydian has a raised fourth degree. In the case of the F Lydian Mode (featured below) the note is a B natural. If we were looking at the F Major scale, the fourth degree would be a B flat (Bb). Below, find the charts with the fingerings and notes for the F Lydian scale, starting from the fifth string.

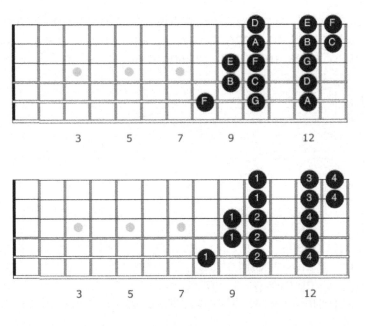

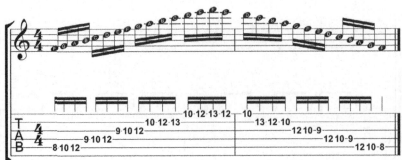

Lesson #67: Lydian Mode Licks

The Lydian Mode is a very bright and jazzy sounding Major-type scale. Here are three licks based on the F Lydian. They can be used over F Major harmonies.

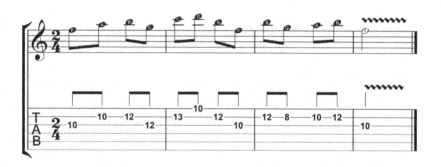

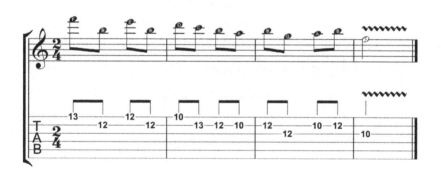

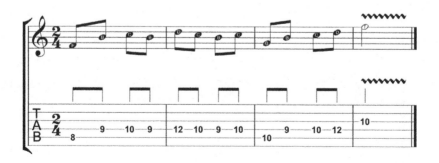

Lesson #68: Some More Lydian Licks: C Lydian

Here are some more Lydian Mode licks that you can use in your playing. These are based on the C scale, whose root note is on the third fret of the fifth string. Try these licks over C Major or C Major Seven chords to give a slightly exotic sound to your melodic playing.

The sharp fourth degree (F# in these examples) of the scale gives the Lydian its most defining characteristic.

Explore the ideas in these licks and try developing some guitar licks of your own, using the Lydian scale. Try slightly changing the order of the notes in these licks or add a few slides (up or down). You might also try to change the rhythm of some of the notes in each lick, making the musical phrase move a little faster or slower.

Have Fun!

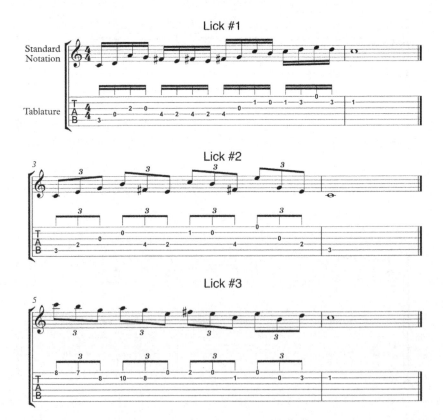

Lesson #69: Mixolydian Mode from the 5th String: Three Notes Per String (3NPS)

The Mixolydian Mode is very similar to the Major Scale in many respects. However, the main difference is that the seventh note of the Mixolydian is a half step lower than the Major Scale. This lower seventh note gives the Mixolydian a bluesy quality. As you are practicing this scale, listen to the sound of the F going to the G, or the reverse. This is the sound of the flat seventh, which gives the scale its characteristic sound.

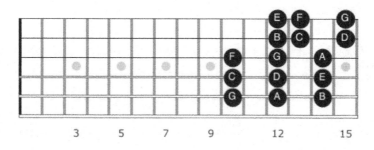

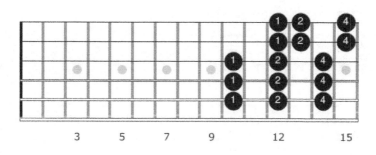

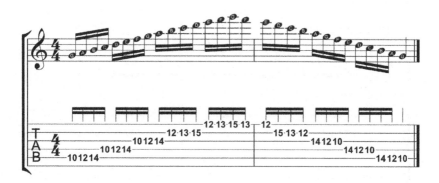

75

Lesson #70: Mixolydian Mode Licks

The following three licks use the Mixolydian Mode. You can use these licks or variations on them over G Major, G7, or G9 chords. They also work well over a I, IV, V Progression (or similar chord progression in the key of G or C). Take your time exploring their sounds and Have fun!

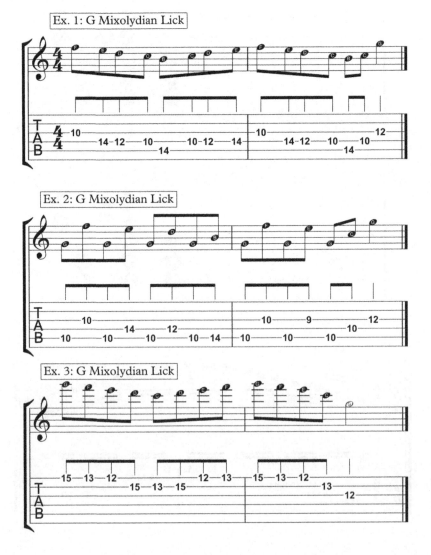

Lesson #71: Aeolian Mode (Minor Scale) from the 5th String: Three Notes Per String (3NPS)

In Lesson #24, we learned the A Minor scale in open position. In this lesson, in some ways, things have come full circle. We are now playing the A Minor scale (otherwise known as the Aeolian Mode) on the 12th fret. The 12th fret is where the open-string notes repeat (or return, depending on one's perspective) one octave higher. In other words, the open A note that starts the scale in Lesson #24 is the A on the 12th fret of the 5th string, but one octave higher. Congratulations on your progress and good work!

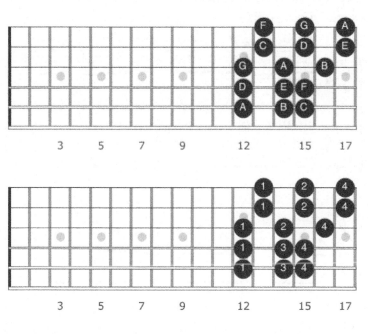

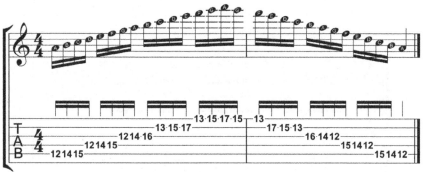

Lesson #72: Aeolian Mode Licks

In these three licks, we are going to outline characteristics of the Minor Scale. The first example uses a neoclassical technique. The second example outlines the A Minor arpeggio (the notes A, C, and E). The third example uses a descending sequence of notes from the scale.

In music, a sequence is a repeated pattern over different notes. The effect is something that sounds a little bit the same and a little bit different. Sequences can be used with any scale. They can be a great way to build up energy during a crescendo. However, just be mindful not to use too many sequences in a row. After about three or four sequences, without variation, they can start to sound a bit repetitive.

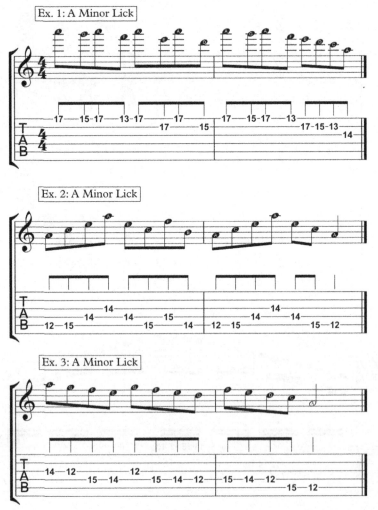

Lesson #73: Listening to yourself and others

Every few days or once a week, record yourself playing some of your favorite songs or licks. You don't need to have an expensive recording device. If you have a microphone and some dictation or recording software on your phone, tablet or computer, those will work as well.

These recordings do not need to be high fidelity. The purpose of recording yourself is to listen to your playing from an "outside" perspective. When you press the playback, pay attention to your rhythm, the evenness of your tone and playing, and your expression. Every week, try to make slight improvements in these areas.

Have a positive and constructive attitude when you are listening to these recordings. Try not to get hung up on small details or little mistakes. Instead, listen to any awkward patterns or habits in your playing and work on improving in those areas.

As a side benefit, this practice will also get you used to the process of recording. So, if you are ever in a recording studio or at a friend's house making a recording, the process will not feel that unusual to you. You will be right at home.

This week, as you work on improving your guitar playing and musicianship, have a little fun by listening to some genres and styles of music outside of your regular listening comfort zone. The best musicians often have a broad knowledge of music and can draw inspiration from many styles.

By exposing yourself to new artists and genres, you will grow in new and unexpected ways as a guitarist. For instance, if you are a Blues fan and try listening to a few Classical recordings, you might get some new ideas for sound colors and textures on the electric guitar. If you are a Metal player and listen to some Jazz recordings, you might get some new ideas for riffs and rhythms.

Lesson #74: Guitar Technique: Hammer Ons

Check Out Video Lesson 10: Hammer Ons

Hammer ons are almost the opposite of pull offs. They are a technique where you bring a finger in your left hand down quickly on a fret without plucking the string with your right hand. This technique can be done with any finger of the left hand; however, it is easiest to execute with the index finger. For hammer ons, it is very important to use the tip of your left-hand finger as the striking surface on the string. This will ensure that the sound is very resonant and well formed. Also, to create effective hammer ons, it is more important to use speed, rather than power, with the motion of your left-hand finger. It should come down on a fret with a fast, but not too powerful, hammer-like motion. The corresponding video on hammer ons will give you a good idea about how to play them and how they sound.

 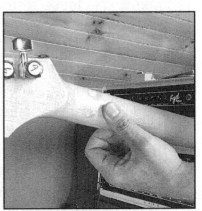

These illustrations show good hammer-on technique.

Give these hammer ons on the High E string a try.

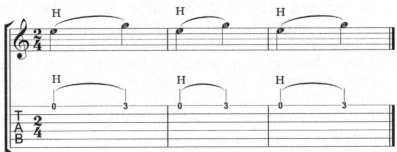

Lesson #75: Hammer On Licks

Here is a hammer-on lick that you can use over E Major. You might try repeating the figure a few times to create more energy and a crescendo in the musical phrase.

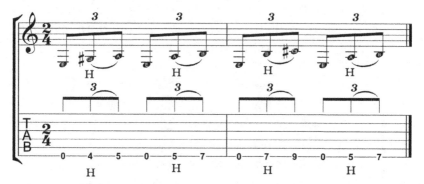

Here is a triplet figure (example #2) that would work well over E Minor. The sound of the lower strings, especially when there is an open low E note, can give a dramatic and ominous sensibility to the musical phrase or song.

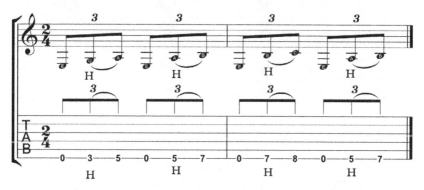

The last lick (in A Pentatonic Minor) works with Blues in A.

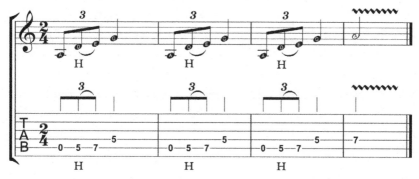

Lesson #76: The Locrian Mode

The Locrian Mode is the most "outside" and exotic sounding of the Modes. It has a dissonant sound with a lot of flat scale degrees: b2, b3, b5, b6, and b7. The Locrian Mode makes appearances in Jazz and Metal genres, as well as film and television scores (especially when a scene requires a musical atmosphere evoking something strange, otherworldly, or sinister.)

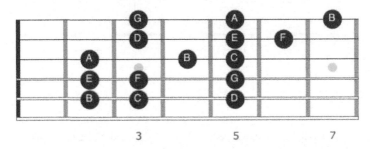

Above and below are the notes and fingerings.

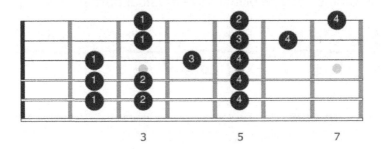

Below, please find the standard notation and the tablature for the B Locrian Mode in two octaves.

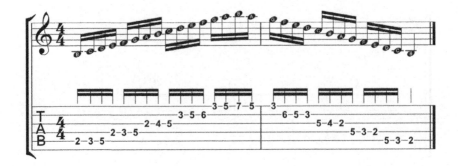

Lesson #77: Locrian Mode Licks

We have some Locrian licks (a little bit exotic sounding), which use hammer ons and pull offs. If you like the sound of the Locrian Mode, you might listen to some of Joe Satriani's music. He is a master of modal inventiveness.

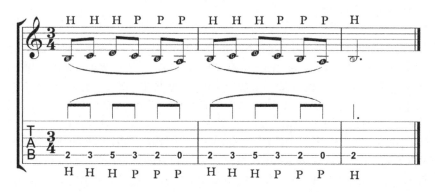

This is an especially fun one, which slithers its way from a low B up an octave. Explore the legato sound.

Lesson #78: Creating Guitar Solos

Creating a guitar solo is like composing some music on the spot. Great guitarists seem to be in the moment as they improvise. Even though they have some licks and stylistic flourishes that they play, they also bring in something that is new and vibrant.

When you create your guitar solos you might also consider to act, in a way like a musical storyteller. For your solo, you might try to make a beginning, middle and end. At the beginning of your solo, you might take some notes or phrases from the melody of the song. The audience's ears will pick up on this and be curious. Then, start to add some notes or rhythms that are not part of the melody. As you do this, you might also add a little tension by moving to higher notes on the guitar. By using some of the techniques that you have learned from this book, like bends, hammer ons and pull offs, slides, and vibrato, you can add interest and variety to your solo. Then, you should strive to reach the pinnacle note of your solo. This does not need to be the highest note of your solo; however, it should probably be a note related to the main chords (most likely the root note) of the song. Then, as an ending, you might create a little outro: a kind of closing statement where the guitar fades back into the texture of the song.

This story-telling approach to guitar solos is a good first step, and, as most techniques in this book, it is a starting point for you to explore musical ideas. One thing that you might consider with this approach is the emotional trajectory of your solo. For example, you might start things out quietly with some slow, repeated notes and then build up to some fiery high notes and string bends. Another approach would be to start things out with a roar and some wild playing and then gradually simmer things down or make a transition to a happier range of expression. The choice is yours here. That's what makes things fun and interesting. Do your best to explore your creativity and your own musical voice.

Lesson #79: Learning the Notes of the Fretboard: The Fourth String: D

In this lesson, let's take a look at the notes of the D string. The D string is an interior string. Oftentimes, guitarists learn the note names on the outer strings —the Low E, A, B, and High E—but don't get around to learning the notes on the G and D strings. Having a knowledge of these interior strings will greatly help you in building fluency throughout the guitar neck. It will also ensure that you don't have any gaps in your understanding of the landscape of the fretboard.

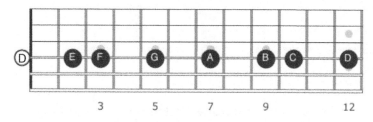

Above, find the natural notes on the D string.
Below, find the sharp notes on the D string.

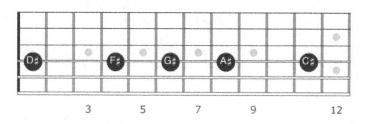

Below, find the flat notes of the D string. Remember that the notes on the fretboard all repeat, starting at the 12 fret. This is true for all of the guitar strings.

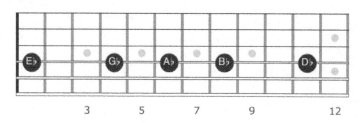

Lesson #80: The Blues Scale

The Blues scale is just the Minor Pentatonic scale with an added flat fifth above the root. In the case of the A Pentatonic Minor, the note would be Eb. In the scale charts below, we have the A Minor Pentatonic (the scale without the Eb) and the A Blues scale (the one with Eb).

A Pentatonic Minor

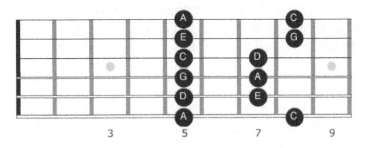

A Blues Scale

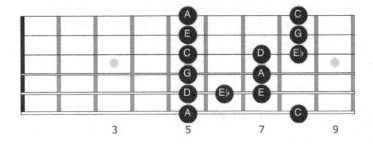

Play through these two scales and listen to the slight difference in sound. The Eb, for lack of better words, gives the scale its Blues sound. A common melodic move is to go from the Eb to the E like this:

86

Lesson #81: Blues Scale Licks

Melodies and licks from the Blues scale work well over dominant seventh chords—like A7, D7, and E7. The scale also works well over minor seventh chords—like Fm7, Gm7, and Em7. The licks on this page are in the key of A and can be played over Blues or Minor Blues in A. They can also be used in the context of a I, IV, V (or similar chord progression) in A Major or A Minor, to give things a Blues-sounding feel. Have fun exploring these!

This classic Blues lick uses whole-step bends from D to E and then walks down the scale chromatically to the A.

This Blues lick, which also uses triplet rhythms, dives right in by going from the A (the root note of the scale) to the Eb (the flat 5th of the scale) in the first two notes. Feel free to add your own expressions to the riff.

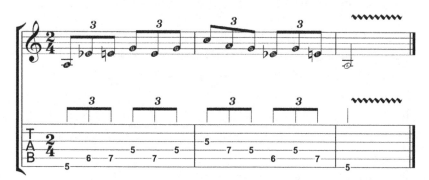

Lesson #82: More Blues Licks

Here are three Blues licks in A. They all feature triplet rhythms and a fair sprinkling of b5 (Eb) notes.

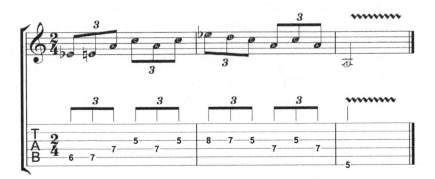

The first two wriggle up and down, respectively, to the A root note. Once you have learned the licks, try adding slides, pull offs, and hammer ons to the mix.

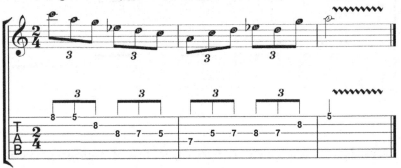

The last Blues lick on the page uses pull offs on the 5th string. It could be used in a Hard Rock context to give a Blues feel, similar to Joe Satriani open-string pull offs.

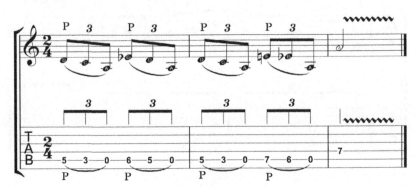

Lesson #83: Pentatonic Major Scale

There are two easy ways to think about the Pentatonic Major scale. The first is that it is a Major scale, but without the fourth and seventh degrees. In other words, the scale is formed like this: I, II, III, V, VI. In the key of C Major it would have these notes: C, D, E, G, and A. The second way is to think of it as Mode 2 of the Minor Pentatonic scale. In the charts below, you will find the notes and fingerings for the C Pentatonic Major.

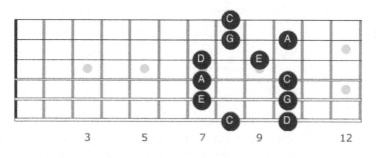

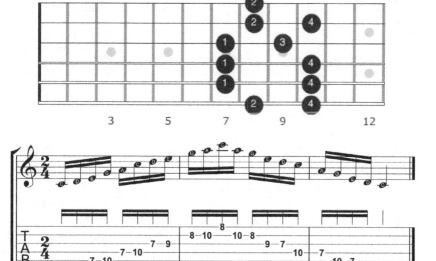

The Pentatonic Major is a great scale for improvising and guitar solos, especially over Major chord progressions or Blues. There aren't a lot of "wrong notes" in the scale.

Lesson #84: Pentatonic Major Licks

Guitarists often add the b3 (in this case, the Eb) to Pentatonic Major licks. This gives the phrase a Country or Bluegrass sound. Like the lick below, you might slide up or down from the b3 (the Eb).

This second lick also uses idiomatic slides from the b3 (Eb) notes. Once you learn the lick, try to move it around to other common guitar keys, like G, A, D, E, and F.

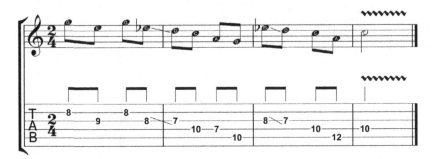

This next lick has wider intervals and a few string skips. It would be a great lick to close out a solo or as a fill in a Country or Bluegrass song.

Lesson #85: Learning the Notes of the Fretboard: The Fifth String: A

Learning the notes of the A string is crucial for advancing on guitar, since so many scales and chords have their root or bass notes (in the case of chords) on the fifth string. As with all of the fretboard memorization in this book, spend some time with each chart, playing the notes on your guitar neck and saying the note names.

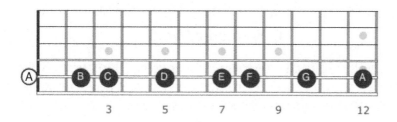

The chart above covers the natural notes on the A string (the fifth string) of the guitar.

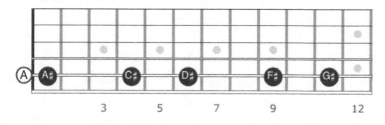

The chart above covers the sharp notes on the A string (the fifth string) of the guitar. The chart below covers the flat notes on the A string (fifth string) of the guitar neck.

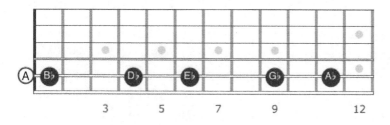

Advanced Level:
Lesson #86: Harmonic Minor Scale

There are two other common forms of the Minor Scale: the Harmonic Minor and Melodic Minor Scales. The Harmonic Minor Scale is just like the Natural Minor Scale (a "fancy" name for the Minor Scale), except that between Scale Degrees 6 and 7 there is both a Whole and Half Step. There is also a Half Step between Scale Degrees 7 and 8.

Here are two scale charts for the C Harmonic Minor scale.

C Harmonic Minor

A strong characteristic of this scale is the sounds from Ab to B to C. As you are learning the scale, pay particular attention to the sounds of these three notes.

The diagram below gives you the finger pattern for the scale. Pay special attention to the notes on the second string: Ab, B, and C. There is a fairly big finger span between the Ab and B (frets 9 and 12). Take your time to get a sense of the distance and finger stretch between these two notes. It is a good idea to isolate this section of the scale and practice playing Ab to B, Ab to B to C, or the reverse C to B to Ab. Start slowly and gradually add speed.

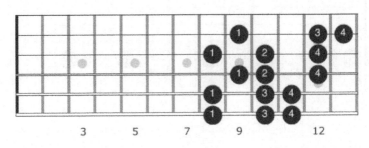

Lesson #87: Harmonic Minor Scale Licks

Here are four licks in C Harmonic Minor that are in a Neoclassical style. They can be used in C Minor.

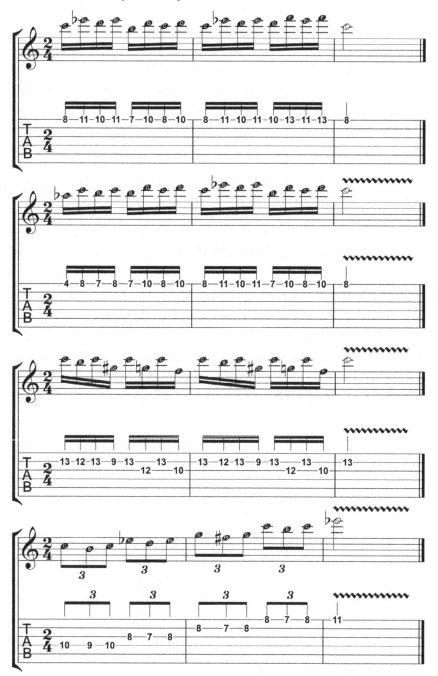

Lesson #88: Melodic Minor Scale

The Melodic Minor scale is similar to the Minor scale (Natural Minor scale), except that for scale degrees 6 and 7 it follows the format for the Major scale. For this reason, the Melodic Minor scale is sometimes called the "Ionian Flat 3" scale. The scale form for the Melodic Minor that we are going to look at here is the one used in Jazz, Fusion, and Rock. In Classical music, the Melodic Minor is a little bit different descending (going down); in Classical music it turns into the Natural Minor scale descending. However, in this book we are going to present the form that is commonly used in Jazz, Rock, and Metal playing; this form stays the same going up and down (ascending and descending).

Melodic Minor

The Melodic Minor Scale (ascending) is just like the Natural Minor Scale, except that between scale degrees 6 and 7 it is the same as the Major Scale.

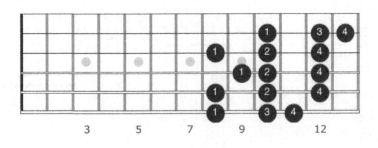

Lesson #89: Licks with Minor Scales

Here are three licks that use the C minor scales. Each one uses open strings to help you change positions on the guitar neck quickly. After you learn them, take a little time to explore making variations on each lick: add slides and bends.

If you haven't done so already, take a moment to check out the video lessons on the Steeplechasemusic.com webpage for *Guitar Scales Handbook*. These videos will further elaborate on the concepts presented in the book and show you some new techniques, licks, and theory .

Also, try some of the minor licks from the bonus lessons.

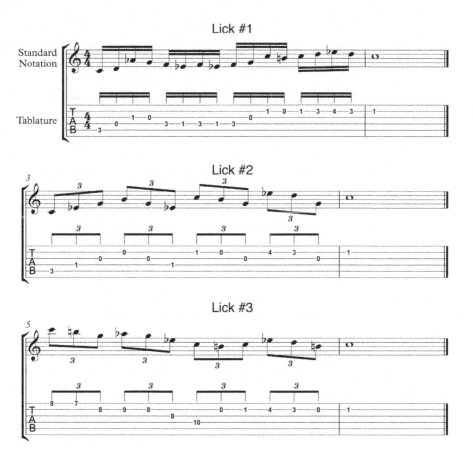

Lick #1

Lick #2

Lick #3

Lesson #90: Learning the Notes of the Fretboard: The Sixth String: Low E

Congratulations! We are on the final string of the guitar for our fretboard memorization. At this point in your studies of the fretboard you should be seeing, hearing, and feeling patterns horizontally up and down the guitar neck. As well, you should also be beginning to pick up patterns that move vertically: from string to string; for example, you might notice that the pitch for the open High E string could also be played in these fretboard locations: B string 5th fret, G string 9th fret, D string 14th fret, and A string 19th fret.

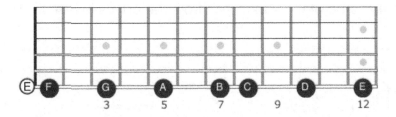

Above, are the natural notes for the Low E string. Below, are the sharp notes for the Low E string.

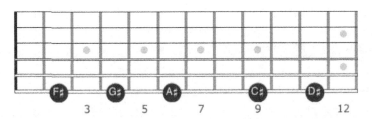

Below, are the flat notes for the Low E. All of these notes (the naturals, sharps, and flats) are the same notes as the High E string, but two octaves lower.

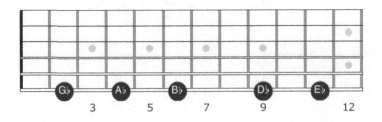

Lesson #91: Major Scale & Modes from the Sixth String

In the following pages, we are going to look at three-note-per-string (3NPS) shapes for the Major scale and Modes starting on the sixth string (the Low E string).

These scale forms, like almost all of the scales forms presented in this book, are moveable, meaning that you can use the same finger pattern and shift it to different keys by starting on a different root note on the fretboard. For example, we are going to use the F Major scale, which starts on the first fret of the sixth string as our root note. However, you could play an A Major scale simply by moving your index finger up to the fifth fret of the sixth string and playing the same finger pattern as you played for the F Major scale on the first fret of the sixth string. You can use this easy method to play all of these scales and modes in all of the keys.

F Major Scale (Ionian Mode)

Here are the notes and fingerings for the F Major scale in three-note-per-string (3NPS) format.

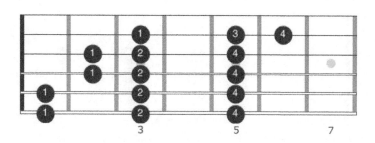

Lesson #92: G Dorian & A Phrygian Modes from the Sixth String: Three-Notes-Per-String (3NPS)

The first two scale charts on this page are for the G Dorian Mode. Just a reminder, all of the 3NPS forms from this section are moveable, meaning you can play the pattern in any key just by moving to a different fret.

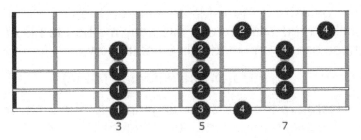

The two charts below are for the A Phrygian Mode.

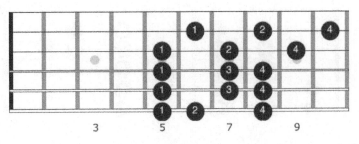

Lesson #93: Legato Playing & Licks
with Dorian and Phrygian Modes

For legato playing, give a strong pick stroke on the first note of the phrase (see the indications in the lick examples below). Play with the finger tips of your left hand and make smooth and connected pull offs and hammer ons. Try to make the notes blend slightly.

This first lick is in G Dorian and can be played over G Minor.

The next lick is in A Phrygian and can be played over A Minor.

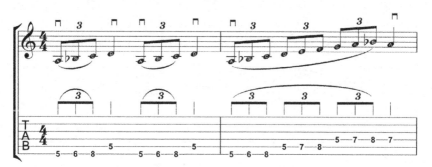

The 3rd lick is in A Phrygian and can be played over A Minor.

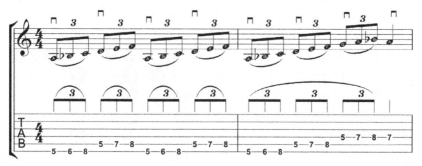

Lesson #94: Bb Lydian & C Mixolydian Modes from the Sixth String (3NPS)

In the first two scale charts, you will find the Bb Lydian scale starting from the sixth string. This moveable scale form can be used over Major chords to get a bright sound.

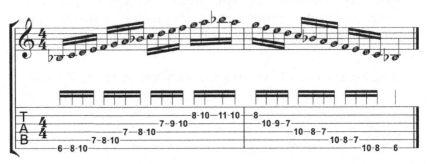

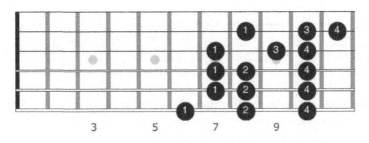

The next two scale charts are for the C Mixolydian scale.

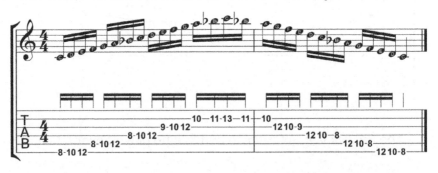

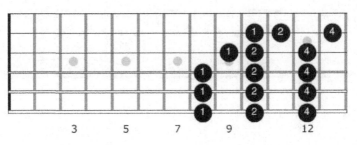

Lesson #95: Lydian & Mixolydian Mode Licks with Sequences

Sequences are patterns in music where the basic pattern sounds the same, but the notes change. Sequences are a great technique to help build up the excitement in your playing. However, try not to use too many of them in a row. If you use more than four sequences in a row, the music can sound a little bit predictable and boring.

Below are some sequences in Lydian and Mixolydian:

Here is a Bb Lydian lick that can be played over Bb Major.

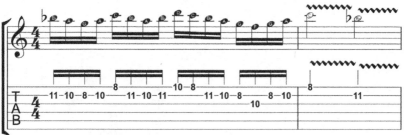

Here is a C Mixolydian lick that can be played over C Major.

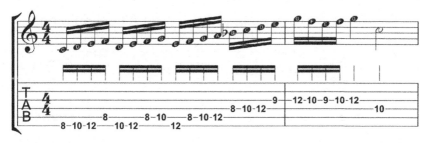

Here is a C Mixolydian lick that can be played over C Major.

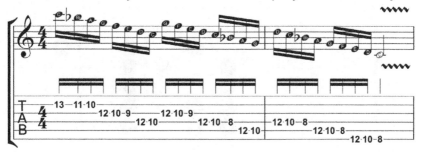

Lesson #96: D Aeolian and A Locrian Modes from the Sixth String (3NPS)

The first two scale charts are for the D Aeolian Mode (also known as the D Minor Scale).

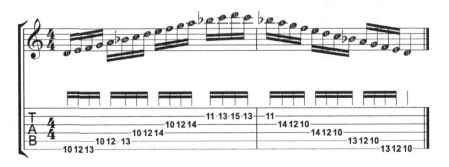

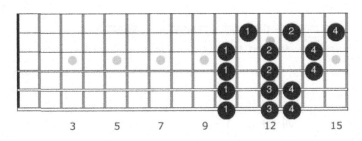

These next two charts are for the A Locrian Mode.

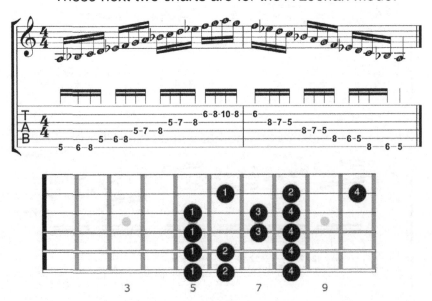

Lesson #97: Speed Picking, Part 1

We are going to work on the speed of our alternate picking in this lesson. The first two examples use triplets on the 6th and 5th strings. Please start with your metronome set to around 60. As you develop accuracy with your alternate picking, gradually set your metronome for a slightly faster tempo. Also, try to use a clean sound.

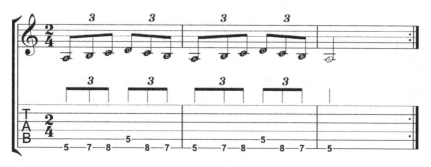

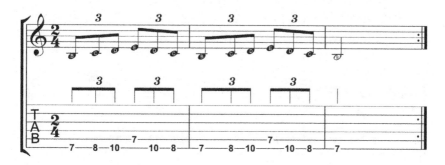

This third example combines the two previous examples. Play it through once, aiming for total accuracy. Then, take a ten-second break, shake your hands and arms out and try it again. Play this between 10 and 20 times in a row.

Lesson #98: Speed Picking, Part 2

A lot of improvements in playing fast on the guitar are made with short bursts of notes: think sprinting rather than marathon running. In the first example, we are going to play six notes, then rest and play the figure again. Please set your metronome for a moderate tempo and gradually, over time, increase the speed.

In this next drill, we are going to add nine notes to the burst. This figure is an ascending scale passage. Try it slowly, then build up the speed.

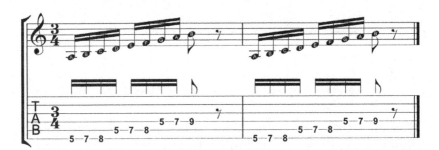

The final drill on this page is ascending and descending. "Spring into action" for the lick, then rest for two beats and play it again. Try it slowly, then build up the speed.

Lesson #99: Speed Picking, Part 3

These next three speed-building exercises follow up on the ideas from the previous page, especially in terms of bursts of nerve and muscle activity.

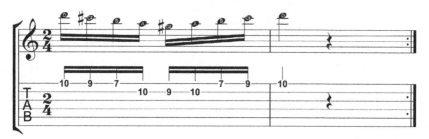

One thing that you may try adding to your picking is to let the pick "give" a little bit as it plucks the string. At high velocity, this may help your hands remain relaxed. Try playing with different amounts of grip strength on the pick.

The third exercise combines the previous two exercises.

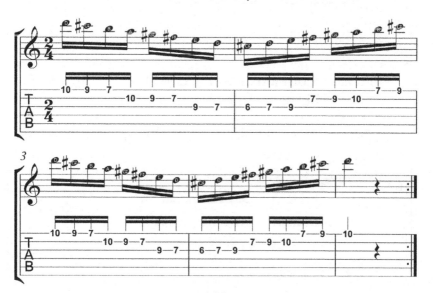

Lesson #100: Using Chord Tones in Your Solos

Using chord tones is a great way to give some harmonic anchors to your guitar solos and improvising. In a nutshell, chord-tone soloing means that you will play notes from the harmony of the music on the main beats of the measures in the song. This will give you and the listeners musical guideposts. (Thing can get more elaborate than this, but this is the basic concept.)

Below, is the C-Major-Scale shape from earlier in the book. The white circles are the chord tones .

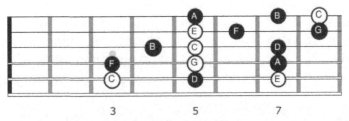

Here is a lick using chord tones in C Major. The circled notes are the chord tones. Notice that they land on the downbeats of the measures.

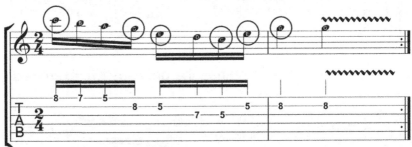

Here is a chord-tone lick that goes from C Major to F Major and then back to C Major.

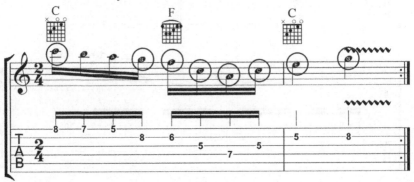

Bonus Lessons: Lesson #101:
CAGED System Overview

The CAGED system is a useful system of note patterns on the guitar fretboard. The system is based on the open C, A, G, E, and D Major chords (pictured below). Over the next few pages, we are going to learn some common and useful patterns for the Major scale and Modes, based on CAGED fingerings. These are close fingerings; so your left hand fingers don't need to span wide distances. However, there is not a uniformity of notes per string, like the 3NPS system. So the right hand has to work a little bit harder. Here are the open-position chords that are the basis for the CAGED system:

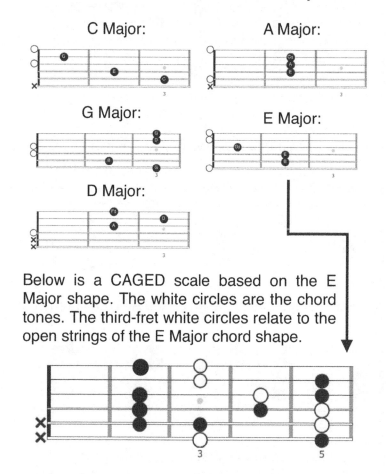

Below is a CAGED scale based on the E Major shape. The white circles are the chord tones. The third-fret white circles relate to the open strings of the E Major chord shape.

Bonus Lessons: Lesson #102:
CAGED System Mode Forms, Part 1

Here are some scales in the CAGED system. The first one is a G Major scale that is based on the E Major chord shape. (See the chord shapes on the previous page.)

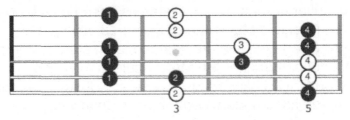

Here is C Major scale that is based on the A Major chord shape. (See the chord shapes on the previous page.)

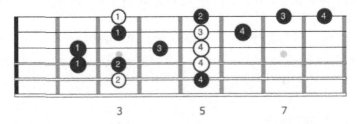

Here is G Minor scale that is based on the E Minor chord shape.

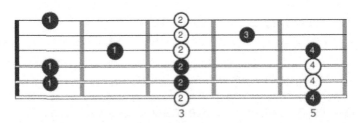

Here is C Minor scale that is based on the A Minor chord shape.

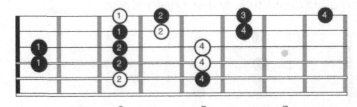

We go into a lot more detail about the CAGED system in the *Ultimate Guitar Chords, Scales & Arpeggios Handbook.*

Bonus Lessons: Lesson #103:
Exotic Scales: The Whole Tone Scale

The Whole Tone scale is used often in Jazz, Classical, and Fusion styles. It is a symmetrical scale, where the notes only move up or down by a whole step distance. Because of this structure, the scale has a "weightless quality" that allows you to land on any note. You can use the whole tone scale over augmented chords (and sometimes Major chords—depending on how "outside" a sound you want to generate).

The two charts below show the A Whole Tone scale.

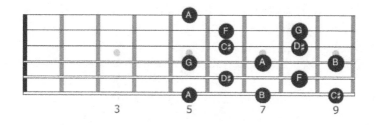

Here is an angular, whole-tone lick that could be used over an A Augmented chord.

Bonus Lessons: Lesson #104:
Exotic Scales: Phrygian Dominant Scale

The Phrygian Dominant is the scale built on the fifth degree of the Harmonic Minor scale. It works very well over dominant harmonies, like an A7 chord. The scale has something of a gypsy feeling, due to the b2 and b6 scale degrees.

In the charts below, you will find the scale pattern and fingering for the A Phrygian Dominant scale. Take your time to explore the unusual tonalities that it can create.

A Phrygian Dominant Scale

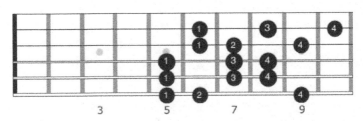

Here is a lick that uses the A Phrygian Dominant scale; it mixes chord tones and non-chord tones and can be played over an A7 chord or other dominant harmonies in A.

Bonus Lessons: Lesson #105:
Exotic Scales: Chromatic Scale

The chromatic scale is a four-note-per-string scale that includes all of the twelve pitches, played ascending or descending in half steps. For example, in the key of A it would be A, Bb, B, C, C#, D, Eb, E, F, F#, G, G#, A.

It's rare that one plays the entire chromatic scale all at once; though it does make an impressive musical flourish. The scale is used more frequently in little sections to link one musical idea or phrase to another.

Also, the scale is a very good warm-up for the fingers, since it uses all four fingers of the left hand. When using it as a warm-up, try playing five-note sequences. This would be the notes on one full string and the next note in the scale on an adjacent string, for example: on the Low E string (ascending) A, Bb, B, C, C# or on the High E string (descending) G#, G, F#, F, E.

In the passage below, please note that you will go from the fourth finger to the first finger on the very highest notes of the scale: G# and A. After you have practiced these sequences, find some of your own.

Chromatic Scale in A

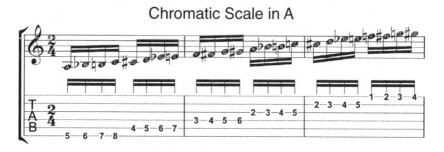

Bonus Lessons: Lesson #106:
Four-Note-Per-String Major & Minor Scale

The final lesson in this book involves four-note-per-string scales. We are going to look at the Major scale (the first chart) and the Minor scale (the second chart). Each of these scales uses all four left-hand fingers on each string. I have added two additional scale notes—the A and B in Major and the A and Bb in Minor—to round things out.

When you are learning these scales, work on one string at a time, starting from the Low-E string. Take your time to feel the distances between each finger. When you are able to play one string comfortably, learn the notes on the A string. Then put the notes

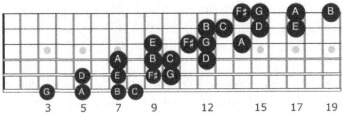

of the Low-E and A strings together, slowly. You might notice that the finger patterns are the same for the Low-E string and the A string on the Major scale. Remember to use a metronome and set it for a slow tempo as you begin your technique drills. After a few weeks, gradually speed up the tempo on the metronome. Remember to play with relaxed, but active hands and arms. It is important that your

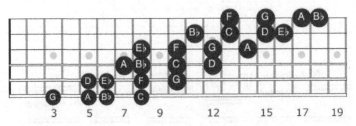

muscles remain relatively relaxed as you play, rather than becoming stiff and rigid.

Congratulations!
You Finished the Book!

Great work in completing this book and video course on scales and guitar technique. You have now developed a very good understanding of the fundamentals guitar playing: major and minor scales, string bending, modes, hammer ons, pull offs, slides, the Blues scale, 3NPS scales, basic music theory, the notes on the guitar neck, picking techniques, and vibrato. You are now able to apply this musical knowledge of the guitar to the songs that you play.

You can sign up for free guitar lessons in your inbox at www.steeplechasemusic.com.

If you would like to continue from here, I would suggest checking out my book, the *Ultimate Guitar Chords, Scales, and Arpeggios Handbook,* which builds on the concepts articulated in this volume.

Keep up the good work and continue to practice the guitar!

Damon Ferrante

About the Author: Damon Ferrante is a Simkins Award-winning composer, guitarist, and music writer. He has had performances throughout the US, Europe, and Asia, most notably, Carnegie Hall, Symphony Space, and Guild Hall. Deeply committed to artistic collaboration, Ferrante has worked with world-class instrumentalists, singers, poets, dance companies, visual artists, and theater companies. For more information on his music, check out: www.DamonFerrante.com.

Check out these books,
Also by Damon Ferrante:

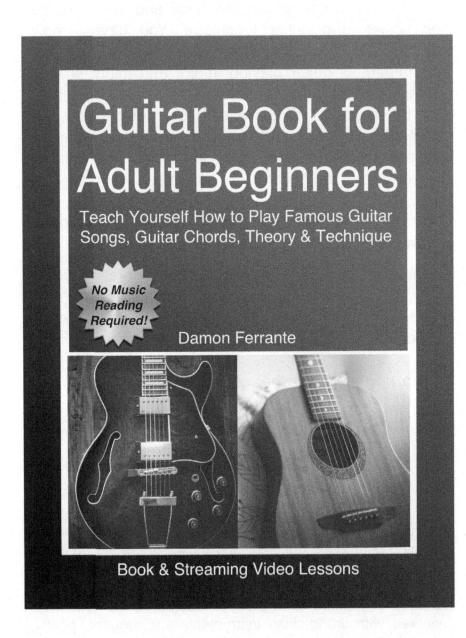

Piano Book for Adult Beginners

Teach Yourself How to Play Famous Piano Songs, Read Music, Theory & Technique

No Music Reading Required!

Damon Ferrante

Book & Streaming Video Lessons

Good News: Bonus lessons!

This edition of *The Guitar Scales Handbook* includes free, bonus lessons. Go to the Home Page of SteeplechaseMusic.com. At the top of the Home Page, you will see a link for Guitar Books. Follow the link to the Guitar Books webpage. Then, click on the link for *The Guitar Scales Handbook.* Once you are on the webpage for the book, click Bonus Lessons and download the PDF and MP3 Audio Files

Have Fun!

Guitar Scales Handbok: A Step-By-Step, 100-Lesson Guide to Scales, Music Theory, and Fretboard Theory (Book & Videos)

by Damon Ferrante

For additional information about music books, recordings, and concerts, please visit the Steeplechase website: www.steeplechasemusic.com

ISBN-13:
978-0615709192 (Steeplechase Arts)

ISBN-10:
0615709192

steepLechase
arts & productions

We want to help you become the guitarist of your dreams!

Check Out Steeplechasemusic.com for Free Guitar Lessons in Your Inbox!

Made in the USA
Monee, IL
01 October 2021